INVALUABLE

MASTER THE 10 SKILLS YOU NEED TO SKYROCKET YOUR CAREER

MAYA GROSSMAN

Invaluable: Master the 10 Skills You Need to Skyrocket Your Career

Copyright © 2020 by Maya Grossman

All rights reserved.

ISBN: 978-1-7354363-0-2

No part of this publication may be reproduced, distributed or transmitted in any form or by any means, including photocopying, recording, or other electronic or mechanical methods, without the prior written permission of the publisher, except in the case of brief quotations embodied in critical reviews and certain other noncommercial uses permitted by copyright law.

Cover creation courtesy of Ravi Verma from rdezines

Editing courtesy of Lorraine Reguly from WordingWell.com

You Might Want to Read This...

As you will soon find out, I'm a very practical person.

I hate it when people talk at a high level and share "inspirational" advice you have no idea how to implement. That is why I made sure this book is as practical as possible.

This book features:

- Full chapters
- Step-by-step guidelines
- Chapter checklist and summary

A complimentary toolkit: The Career Roadmap, available for download from my website: www.mayagrossman.com/resources

I hope you enjoy it!

Table of Contents

Introduction 1

Chapter 1: Skill #1—Develop an Owner Mentality 13

Chapter 2: Skill #2—Become a Lifelong Learner 39

Chapter 3: Skill #3—Focus on Making an Impact 65

Chapter 4: Skill #4—Be an Opportunity-Digger 83

Chapter 5: Skill #5—Become a Fixer 97

Chapter 6: Skill #6—Become a Master Influencer 115

Chapter 7: Skill #7—Master the Art of Managing—Up and Across 131

Chapter 8: Skill #8—Extreme Accountability 143

Chapter 9: Skill #9—Become a Planner 157

Chapter 10: Skill #10—Develop the Habit of Tracking Your Success 177

Summary: The Invaluable Mindset—How it All Comes Together.. 183

Thank You 189

Who is Maya Grossman?... 193

Introduction

When I was 25, the CEO of the company I worked for flew the company jet to meet me for lunch and convince me to stay with the company. I wasn't the most senior employee, I wasn't generating the most revenue for the company, but I was an invaluable employee. Why else would someone fly halfway across the country to try and change my mind about leaving?

The meeting took place at a beachside restaurant, the kind that has a very long wine list and a crisp white tablecloth on every table. It was the type of restaurant I couldn't afford at the time.

It was early in the afternoon, so the restaurant was quiet. The lunch rush hour was over and their staff was setting up the dinner service when we sat down.

I was overwhelmed. It was all a bit surreal. At that point, I had already given my notice but I respected the CEO and the executive team, so I was happy to accept the invitation and hear them out.

I expected a business negotiation, but the conversation was friendly. The CEO asked me about my future plans, my ambitions, and my goals. He wanted to know if I could see a future with the company—in any capacity. To my surprise, he made me a dream offer. I could design my own role! I could choose what I wanted to do that would allow me to grow professionally and feel fulfilled.

For a really long time, I was committed to the company and my role. It was my first real job and it was a good one. While most of my friends busted tables to pay for college, I sat in an air-conditioned office, wore pencil skirts and high heels, and got to work with some of the best tech companies in the world. During my seven years with the international company that had over 400 employees, I was able to go from working at a call center (which was one of the most junior roles) to being a manager and reporting to the most senior executive.

When it was time to get my Bachelor's degree, the CEO worked out a special offer for me so that I could take night classes and keep working full-time. They truly went above and beyond for me. I was thankful for those seven years, but I knew it was time for me to move on.

I thanked the CEO for the generous offer and for everything he and his team did for me throughout the years. He understood why I was leaving and he was genuinely happy for me to go do something I loved.

I didn't know it then, but that was my first encounter with great leadership.

I was quite fortunate to have my time with that company be my first real work experience, because it allowed me to set a high standard for what a workplace should be like and how I should be treated as an employee.

I didn't start this book with that story for the dramatic effect, but because I want to make it crystal clear that being an invaluable employee has nothing to do with your profession. It doesn't matter how old you are or where you are starting from. Anyone—yes, anyone, including you—can become an invaluable employee.

When I originally started writing this book, I had a different title in mind. I wanted to call the book *Becoming Exceptional*. The word "exceptional" stuck in my head because one of my managers once told me I was an exceptional employee. It felt like the right word to use to describe an employee who can perform better than others, but I realized that "exceptional" is a relative term. An employee who merely gets the job done at a company or in a workplace where most people slack off could be considered an exceptional employee. By definition, they are the exception to the norm, but that is not the kind of employee I want to empower you to be. This book is about teaching you to think differently about your role as an employee, and equipping you with the skills you need to become invaluable—no matter what you do and who you work for.

Since the word "exceptional" didn't work, I had to find another way to describe what it meant to be an outstanding employee—the kind of employee every company wants to hire and retain, and the kind of employee people talk about years after they leave because they have made a big impact. I wanted to find one word that would instantly make people understand what I'm talking about. That's when I came across the definition of "invaluable."

in·val·u·a·ble

—valuable beyond estimation; priceless.

Bingo!

An invaluable employee is someone who delivers staggering results that have a real impact on the company they work for. An invaluable employee goes beyond *just* getting the job done. They do whatever it takes, including going through brick walls without having to be asked, to achieve whatever goal is in front of them. They find creative solutions, they look to maximize the results of their work, and they solve problems without being prompted to do so. An invaluable employee speaks up. They own up to their mistakes. They are accountable for themselves and for others. They know how to lead without authority and mobilize peers, regardless of their seniority. If there was an Employee Olympics, they would be the gold medalists.

No one is born with all of the skills that make an invaluable employee. Invaluableness is something you develop over time and grow into. Contrary to what we were told our entire lives, we are not born with our talents. We develop them. The ability to succeed in your career or anywhere else is not an innate talent, it's a mindset and a lifestyle you can adopt.

You may not feel like you have it in you just yet, and that's perfectly fine. **Where you are today is not where you are going to stay**. You still have a journey ahead of you and this book is the first step towards realizing your invaluableness. If you give yourself some time, if you invest in yourself, and if you take action, you will get there. You will become an invaluable employee, no matter what your third grade teacher told you or what your colleagues think of your ambitions.

The question is: are you prepared to put in the work? Like everything in life, it's a choice that you need to make. You can choose to do your job and be like 90% of the workforce, doing your nine to five to get a paycheck. But if you actually want to progress in your career, gain more responsibilities, and make a bigger impact, you can't just go through the motions. That will only keep you in place. If you want to move up and acquire more opportunities to learn, you need to take a different approach and deliberately work towards becoming invaluable. I've seen success numerous times with people I've hired and trained as well as colleagues and friends I have mentored. Anyone can become invaluable, if they understand what it takes, they are intentional about it, and they are willing to do the work most people won't do.

And as exciting as it sounds right now, you have to remember the process of growing your invaluableness is going to take time. It's not going to happen overnight. It may seem like people are getting there faster, but that's just because our culture celebrates success and hides failure. You get to see the 1% that made it, not the 99% who are still working toward it.

On a long enough timeline, you can learn anything you need, in order to pursue the career of your dreams. You can take steps to become the person you want to become, if you believe that you can. After all, a human is the ultimate adaptation machine. We are wired to constantly learn and change; it's part of our DNA. Think about it this way: Did you know how to walk when you were born? Did you know how to speak? Did you know how to interpret social cues or control your anger when you were a teenager? Probably not. You learned how to do all of these things. Unlike man-made software, we are not given a set number of features. We learn and grow, every single day of our lives. We can constantly reinvent ourselves and become a better version of ourselves. No one is born with a degree or a profession. Every single person out there had to learn to become who they are. They had to put in the time and the effort, to hone their skills. The great news is that if you start today, tomorrow you'll be one day closer to the finish line.

Some of the tactics in this book may cause your friends or loved ones to raise a brow. It may seem excessive, over the top, or simply ridiculous that you should spend time—a lot of time—on becoming a better version of yourself. I get it. When I first started looking into career development, my family and friends thought I was losing it.

They didn't understand what I was talking about, when I mentioned how I was working on my limiting beliefs and visualizing my goals. They thought everything I was doing to upgrade myself was weird. I admit, it was different. It wasn't what everyone else was doing, but that was the whole point!

You can read this book cover to cover and never live up to your potential if you don't believe you can become invaluable. No matter how tactical the advice I share is, if you don't think you can become an invaluable employee, you probably won't become one. Now, this isn't about what other people think, it's about what you believe. Everyone around you may think you don't have what it takes and they will be wrong, but if you don't believe you have it in you, you'll be right. As one of my favorite fitness gurus, Jillian Michaels, says in her workout videos, "What you believe, you achieve." Let me tell you something: she is right!

Unfortunately, most people don't believe they can become invaluable. They wake up every morning, go to a job they hate, fill their time with endless distractions, and go home with a paycheck, feeling sorry for themselves. It's not that they don't have the potential to become invaluable, because they do. What they don't realize is that they have the power to make their career meaningful. They *can* decide what their day-to-day would look like, they *can* decide to get a raise or a promotion, and they *can* decide to do work that impacts others, but it's much easier to stay in the gray and go through the motions. Heck, some of the people I worked with turned that into a work of art! They perfected the concept of cruising at work to the point they barely ever had to do anything. Some people think it's an achievement to get away with doing nothing at work, but I consider it one of my worst nightmares.

You picked up this book because you want to be different, because you want to do better, and because you want to become the best version of yourself. You chose to read this book because you know you were meant for more, and that puts you ahead of most people. Let me tell you something, being invaluable feels amazing! It feels like being a real life superhero, minus the cape. Knowing you can make the most incredible things happen at work is a great boost to your confidence and a feeling that will keep you motivated.

You can experience all of that too, so don't live your life according to someone else's plan. Don't let anyone else decide who you should and shouldn't be. What works for them may not be enough for you, and that's fine. It's okay to want more, whatever "more" means to you. You want a job that pays better? Great. You want to try out a new profession? Amazing—go for it. You want to climb the ladder and get that title? Respect. You want to lead others? That's inspiring.

You get to decide what the best version of yourself looks like because you are the one who is going to do the work. Unless your family and friends are in the trenches with you, they don't get a say in your career. No one does.

Instead of focusing on what other people think, focus on the opportunities. It will give you the motivation and the momentum you will need to kick off this process.

Ask yourself: What would happen if it's true, if I can become invaluable? What would my career look like if I get to decide what it looks like? Well, there is only one way to find out.

So, what's the deal with soft skills?

A few years ago, I decided to spend more time coaching and mentoring. I committed to meeting anyone who asked to meet with me that year. I ended up going to 25 meetings with colleagues and marketing professionals who were building their careers. They all wanted to know what my secret was—how I was able to lead a so-called successful career and do meaningful work. As I was answering that question for the millionth time, I realized there was actually a method to my madness. I wasn't making random decisions, nor was I applying a one-off tactic. I was using the same skills again and again to help me make smart decisions, identify opportunities, and deliver outstanding results—regardless of the situation or industry I was working in or the product I was working on. These skills had nothing to do with my professional background and everything to do with mindset. When I looked back on my career, I realized I was invaluable long before I got into marketing. It wasn't about my profession, it was something else entirely—something I finally had a name for: soft skills.

So, what are those skills, exactly? Soft skills are most often referred to as people skills, and include social skills, communication skills, character and/or personality traits, and emotional intelligence, among others. They are the skills that enable you to navigate your environment, work well with others, perform at a high level, and achieve your goals. Unlike your profession or "hard" skills, soft skills are not about the knowledge you have but rather the behaviors you display in different situations and the habits you create for yourself.

The name "soft skills" is quite misleading. It almost sounds like an afterthought. In reality, it's the most important toolbox you can have at your disposal. Soft skills are the ultimate competitive advantage, in life and in work. When you think about it, they are the superpower that makes invaluable employees real-life superheroes.

To be fair, it seems like we would still need hard skills (AKA a profession), in the next decade or so (you know, before every job is automated and the robots take over), but having a profession is not enough. We live in a world that constantly changes. Jobs are created, redesigned, and eliminated at an unprecedented pace. It is hard to keep up. By the time you graduate, the hard skills you acquired in college may no longer be relevant. That is why it is so important to develop a strong foundation with the right soft skills. They won't replace the need for a vocation, but they will give you a toolbox for success in everything you do. When you have the right mindset and the right tools, you can adjust, learn new skills, and figure out how to apply the knowledge you acquired in new ways, so it doesn't matter if your career trajectory changes. Those skills will help you future-proof your career.

Imagine a situation where you are blindfolded and have sound-blocking headphones on. Your left hand is pinching your nose so you can't smell anything. You pick up a spoon and take a bite from whatever is on the plate in front of you. You can eat the food, but without your other senses, you are unable to guess what you are eating. When you are unable to use all five senses, your ability to succeed diminishes.

That is exactly what happens when you only apply hard skills at work. You are ignoring your superpowers and limiting your ability to succeed.

Unlike most of the stuff you learn in school, the more you use and apply your soft skills, the more successful you get. Soft skills provide a foundation for anything you do in life, no matter what you choose as your vocation. Whether you are a kindergarten teacher or a tech executive, mastering the skills in this book would position you in the top 10% of the workforce.

I can't guarantee you'll get the jet and the expensive restaurant, but I can promise you that by the time you finish reading this book and applying what you learn, you'll start reaping the rewards of being an invaluable employee. For me, that meant being promoted 10 times in 15 years, receiving hefty bonuses and raises (mostly without asking), gaining additional experiences that spread beyond my job description, and having fun in the process.

I have had what I define as a challenging yet fulfilling career, and none of it happened by mistake. I worked my butt off to become an invaluable employee, and it was worth it.

This book is not a cheat sheet to success because, unfortunately, there are no shortcuts. If you want to become an invaluable employee, you will need to do the work. The good news is that I compressed 15 years of experience into this book so you don't have to go through the trial and error of figuring it out on your own.

How to Read this Book

This book is laid out in such a way so that it will be easier for you to read it and adopt the different skills. Each new skill you will learn builds on the skills you previously developed, so I recommend reading the book in order—at least, the first time around. If you come back to it for a second or third time, you could read chapters individually and work on perfecting your execution.

The first seven skills (from Chapters 1-7) will teach you the fundamentals of the invaluable mindset so you can start building confidence in your abilities—from developing an owner's mindset to building a growth machine that will keep you learning, to creating your own opportunities and delivering maximum impact.

Chapter 8's skill—accountability—is a combination of everything that this book will teach you. Some people may find it challenging to accept the idea of extreme accountability without learning and developing the first seven skills, so it might be easier to digest if you change your perspective gradually, by adopting one skill at a time and letting each one sink in and become part of your identity. Once you master the first seven skills, accountability will become the obvious next step.

Skills from Chapters 9 and 10—planning and tracking—are more strategic and are meant to help you take action, move forward, and stay the course.

At the end of every chapter, you'll find a *Chapter Checklist and Summary* that will help you move from theory to practice. The inclusion of those resulted from the feedback I received from my beta readers. The following chapters were made as actionable as possible, so you won't have any excuses. You will be able to take what you've learned and apply it in your everyday life. I wanted to make sure that you are going to be able to capitalize on the momentum this book will create for you as you read it and to push you to take the first steps towards becoming invaluable.

Getting Started

The information in this book is based on the experience I gained through my career. The focus is on what helped me achieve my career goals, which got me from who I was at a given time to being the person I needed to be to make it to the next step. I'm not the CEO of a successful company or a self-made billionaire. I'm an employee, like many of you, with an insatiable ambition and a desire to make an impact.

Throughout my 15-year career, I was able to work for companies like Microsoft and Google and strategically level up every time I took on a new role. I've done it while making a difference and became a better version of myself with every role.

You are going to hear about my personal journey and how I've dealt with the day-to-day challenges everyone faces as they become part of the workforce. I'll share my wins and failures. I'll talk about professional excellence as well as personal accountability and work ethics. I'll also provide you with actionable guidelines that could take you from delivering mediocre results to becoming an exceptional performer and an invaluable employee.

Every title you see on my resume started as a goal I wanted to achieve. Each turned into a reality. I know you could do the same, if you are able to follow through with these three steps:

1. Understand and accept that you can become invaluable.
2. Adopt the 10 skills I share in this book, make them your de facto mindset.
3. Take action and put those skills to work in the real world.

From now on, choose to see your career as a tool for self-actualization. Choose to believe that you can design the career of your dreams and choose to deliberately move towards your goals.

Choose to believe you are invaluable and you *will* become invaluable.

Chapter 1
Skill #1—Develop an Owner Mentality

I started college when I was 24. I had no idea what I wanted to focus on; I just knew I had to get a bachelor's degree. I wasn't excited about any of the majors the school had to offer, so I decided to go with a fairly safe bet—business management. It seemed like something that would be versatile enough to open doors and create career opportunities without making me choose then and there what I wanted to do for the rest of my life. When it was time to pick my classes, I chose finance because it seemed like it would be a good skill to have, and marketing because it seemed like fun. Boy, was I right. I hated finance but I fell in love with marketing. I liked it so much that I decided I wanted to work in the marketing field, not just learn about it. I didn't know what a career in marketing could look like but I wanted to find out. At the time, marketing wasn't as segmented as it is today. I only had a couple of options: MarCom (Marketing Communications), copywriting, or advertising. Today, marketers can choose between product marketing, demand generation, digital marketing, growth marketing, communications, PR, event marketing, and probably a few more roles I haven't heard of.

I started researching the two roles I identified, so I could learn more about what my future could look like. This was in the mid-2000s. Social media was just becoming a "thing," Facebook and Twitter were gaining traction, and it grabbed my attention.

I was passionate about social media and made it my mission to get a job in that industry, even though I didn't have any hands-on experience. In order to make up for that, I spent hours learning about social media marketing, I followed thought leaders, and I experimented with my different profiles. I did all of that before I had a concrete opportunity in sight. I learned everything I could learn on my own, even before there was a specific role I could apply for.

I found my first marketing job through Twitter. I was following a few influencers on the platform and one of them, the founder of a social media agency by the name Blonde 2.0, tweeted that they were hiring. I think it took me seven minutes to send them my resume. In my mind, this was the dream job.

Now that I had a real opportunity to land a marketing job, I had to make darn sure I gave it my all. I read every Tweet and every blog post the hiring manager wrote and learned what they cared about the most. I researched the company's target audience—tech startups—and learned about entrepreneurship, venture capital, and the challenges of building a company from the ground up.

Despite the fact I had almost no relevant experience, by the time I got to the interview, I knew more about social media and the startup ecosystem than anyone else. (At least, that's what I thought.) Nevertheless, I was nervous. I was about to meet the real-life influencers I had been following for almost a year. They were the gods of social media, as far as I was concerned. No pressure!

I was sweating through my purple silk top as I waited for the co-founders to come in. The first was a tall, beautiful woman who was so fashionably put together that I was speechless for a few seconds. We started talking and the conversation blew my mind. Finally, I was able to talk about everything I had been "geeking out on" with someone who got it. I was so happy, I forgot it was an interview, until the other co-founder came in.

The interview went well and I was asked to work on an assignment to demonstrate my skills. I was to write a review for Google's latest product—Google Wave (yes, I'm old)—in the form of a blog post. In addition, I was asked to review a client's website and offer improvements for the copy and layout. I spent hours on those tasks. I researched the product for the content piece, then learned about user experience (UX) and calls to action (CTA), so I could review the website in a professional way.

I had never done any of those things before but I knew enough about the industry to figure out where to get the information I needed. I was willing to put in the extra effort because I *really* wanted to get the job. I had a hunch that social media was going to be big, and I wanted to be part of the industry.

I clearly remember the moment I received the call from the founders, who let me know they were going to make an offer. I played it cool, but the minute I hung up the phone, I screamed. I just gotten my first "real" marketing job and I knew it was an opportunity to launch a new career!

I was ready to do whatever it took, to become a social media expert.

When I joined their team, Blonde 2.0 was still a small company who employed only a handful of people, but social media was becoming popular, and we were one of only a few agencies who provided social media services, so we grew fast.

Very quickly, the work became a bit chaotic. The more we grew, the more I noticed things weren't quite right on the operational side. We didn't have processes or templates in place, so there was no consistency in our deliverables. We were focused on growth. Unfortunately, that meant some things were falling through the cracks, and it bothered me. It wasn't my job to think about the bigger picture, but I couldn't look the other way. I felt like it was my duty to find a solution to the problem.

I couldn't stop thinking about the challenges that the company was facing, so I was constantly trying to come up with ideas on how to fix them. Then, one day, I had a *Jerry Maguire* moment. I knew exactly what we needed, so I put together a plan. In order to scale, we needed infrastructure and processes, we had to start defining roles and responsibilities, and we needed alignment across the team. I put all of my ideas in a document so that I could present them as a strategic solution. I even included a few charts, to show I meant business.

I presented to my boss as though I were delivering a State of the Union Address. I was excited and nervous. I felt like I had the solution to a very big problem and I believed I was going to make a big difference.

In fact, I did.

When I was done with the speech, the CEO looked at me and smiled. He really liked my initiative as well as my proposed plan, and he was happy for me to start implementing it immediately, as the new team supervisor.

I was ecstatic. I had just gotten my first leadership role, without even asking! That was a big milestone.

I started with a team of five. By the time I left the company, I led 25 employees.

My achievements occurred all because I was able to see the bigger picture and take actions to solve a problem.

My plan wasn't super sophisticated. What I suggested wasn't rocket science; it was common sense. Every employee in the company could have done the same thing if they wanted to, but no one did. Most people focus on their job and their job alone. It takes an invaluable employee to think differently and adopt what I can now describe as an "owner mentality."

When you have an owner mentality, you take everything you are meant to do and go a step further. Employees with an owner's mindset are loyal and committed to the mission and the team. They also own the vision. They feel personally responsible for everything that is happening in the company, even if it's beyond their scope. Their work isn't limited to merely their job description; they step in and do whatever is needed, whenever they identify an opportunity to help. Because they think like owners, they work for the business, not just for themselves. They don't simply drop their metaphorical pen at 5 PM. They feel responsible for the company's success, so they put the company first and make personal sacrifices without complaining.

Having an owner mentality is one of the most significant determinants of success in anything you do. **People who develop an owner mindset can do things that people with an employee mindset cannot do.** Success has nothing to do with seniority or job title; it has everything to do with how you think.

There's nothing wrong with being a typical employee—the kind that completes assigned tasks and who gets the job done quickly and full-heartedly, but that is a given. After all, employees are paid to do their job and do it well.

The only problem is that typical employees are not invaluable. They deliver exactly what they are asked to and nothing more. They focus on their own narrow point of view, instead of trying to get a glimpse of the big picture.

Let's put this concept to the test. If you want to know if you have an employee mentality or an owner mentality, see how you respond to these questions:

Do you work from nine to five, every weekday, or do you live the company's mission and vision 24/7?

Do you focus on the work you have to do this week or do you think about next month and next year?

Do you try to make clients happy or do you do everything humanly possible to delight them because you know the company depends on it?

Do you work on what's urgent or on what is really important and can provide high leverage?

Do you adjust to fit the company's culture or do you define the culture, through your actions?

Are you reactive or proactive?

Do you stick to a tried-and-true approach or do you find new ways to do things?

Do you try until you fail or do you refuse to accept that failure is not an option?

I know, it's a lot to consider. Why should you invest so much, when you are not actually the owner of the company? You are not going to get the same upside as an owner, so why should you go above and beyond? The answer is quite simple and it is the reason you are reading this book: because you want to be invaluable. You want to rise to the top and maybe, one day, become an owner. You not only want to make an impact, you crave it.

Accepting the notion that you are going to go above and beyond without immediate compensation is the biggest mental hurdle you will need to cross, in order to adopt an owner mentality. It is not easy to make sacrifices now for something that will happen in the future, but that is what it takes.

When you adopt an owner's mindset, you will automatically start paying attention to details and seeing things that someone with an employee mindset can't see. If you pay attention to those details and act on what you see, you'll create a competitive advantage that no amount of hard work can generate. Remember my *Jerry Maguire* moment? I was able to notice a problem that was out of my scope because my brain was open to it. I wasn't asking myself how to be a better employee; I was asking myself what I could do to help the company grow and succeed. I focused on the bigger picture instead of just doing my job.

Anyone can develop an owner's mindset. It is possible because it is not something you are born with. It is a way of thinking and behaving that you can learn.

What comes next is everything you can do to start building that ownership muscle right now.

The Circle of Passion at Work

For some people, going to work is a chore. It's an unpleasant but necessary task they have to do. For others, going to work is a passion. It's something that gives them purpose and motivation.

There are always crappy days, no matter how much you love what you do, but for the most part, people can choose to be engaged at work, or they can mentally check out.

The circle of passion at work is a simple process that is meant to help you develop the habit of being engaged at work. The circle starts with finding meaning or purpose at work, no matter how big or small. Once you are able to find purpose, you'll start taking small actions to reinforce that purpose, then those small actions will produce small wins, which will release hits of dopamine that will make you a bit happier. Since you now know taking action in following your purpose can make you happy, you will continue doing it and even go on to take bigger actions. Before you know it, you will have created the motivation to be engaged at work!

It's a strange concept but when you think about it, this process basically gets you hooked on work. To be honest, it's not that much different than developing the habit of working out or waking up early in the morning. It's all about brain chemistry and figuring out how to get that hit of dopamine that is going to keep you motivated. The more you engage, the more you will enjoy your work, and the more you are motivated to take action (be engaged), the more the cycle will keep repeating itself.

So, how do you go about cultivating that purpose or meaning? It starts with choosing the right company to work for.

Choose the Right Company to Work For

I have a theory that even the greatest marketers can't market everything. Great marketers rely on passion in their work, so it's imperative that they like the product or service they are marketing. I am telling you about this theory because I believe it applies to anyone, not just marketers. When you take a real interest in what you do, the industry you are in, and the product you are working on, you will do a better job.

When considering a new career opportunity, people use different criteria in order to make a decision, from salary and benefits to location and ease of commute to the team they are going to work with. I'm suggesting that you add two more criteria: what the company does and how much you are excited by it. If you can identify with and advocate for what the company does, it will be much easier for you to cultivate purpose and develop the circle of passion at work.

There are times when you can just feel a company is not for you. Something feels fishy, you can't exactly figure out what they do, or you simply get a bad vibe. When you get those feelings, choosing to work for them should be an immediate "no." No good will come out of pursuing that opportunity, trust me.

If you don't say "no" on the spot, you should research the company to try and develop interest. The first thing to do is to check out the company's website, to learn more about what they do. Avoid the temptation to skim through it; actually go deep and engage with the content. Start with the home page and focus on their value proposition. What problem is this company solving? Who are they solving it for? Do you find it interesting? Were you curious enough to keep reading?

From the website, you can jump to their social media channels. You can learn a lot about a company, based on the content they share and the story they are telling.

Next, visit review websites to better understand their product or service. Browsing through customer reviews will show you how valuable it is. You'll learn what people like and don't like about the company and the product or service they provide.

The next step is to learn about the industry, to assess whether it's growing or stagnant. Is there a lot of innovation in the market or is it quite old-fashioned?

Last but not least, does their industry pique your interest? You can find the information you need by reading analyst reports from companies like Gartner and Forrester, listening to earning calls, and researching competitors.

After the initial research ask yourself:

- Do I want to know more?
- Can I see the value or potential of the product or service?
- Does it seem like the market they are in is growing?
- Can I see myself proudly telling people about this company?

If the research process got you curious enough to actually go deeper, you may have hit career gold. You found a company that gets your creative juices flowing. That's a big win for the process of cultivating a purpose at work!

Choosing a company that interests you is one of the best ways to become an invaluable employee. It means you'll have to spend less time looking for incentives. It means you will be naturally curious about the industry and product, so learning will come easier. It also means you'll notice opportunities more easily, because your mind will constantly be looking for information about something you like.

Working for a company you can fall in love with will make it easier for you to think like an owner. You will be engaged and excited. Above all, you will be emotionally invested. That makes a world of difference because it gives you a purpose at work!

Having the freedom to choose the next company you want to work for is a privilege. However, what do you do if you've already made that choice and you are at a job you're not sure how to get excited by?

I didn't start my career in marketing. I was actually working for a travel agency early in my career, before I knew what I wanted to do as a professional. I needed a job so I just said "yes" when that opportunity presented itself. I spent seven years with the travel agency before deciding I wanted to go into marketing.

I didn't choose the travel industry, I wasn't excited about it when I joined the company—partly because I knew nothing about it—but I managed to get myself excited.

I had a choice to make. I could have handled that opportunity like it was a temporary gig that I needed to tolerate, or I could develop interest and make that job something I enjoyed doing.

I decided to give it a chance, so I had to figure out how to fall in love with the travel agency. Luckily for me. I didn't have to go far. I was inspired by the founders and the team I worked with. They lived and breathed the travel industry, and their passion was contagious.

I spent the following seven years learning everything there is to know about the travel industry—the tools and systems travel agents used, the audience the company was serving, and where the market was headed. I kept my interest alive by reading about innovation in travel, engaging with other travel agents, and trying to become the best in the field. At the time, travel became my whole world and it allowed me to be engaged and motivated at work.

Cultivate Passion for the Company You Work For

I'm sure you have heard this before. I know I have. A company is not your family. A company is not your friend. Even if you have a lot of friends who work there, even if you have managers and colleagues that you enjoy spending time with, at the end of the day, a company is a business that is driven by the desire to generate revenue, not the desire to make you happy.

It is true. Companies care about their own success. So, why am I telling you to care about the company you work for and cultivate a real passion for what they do? Ah, it is because companies are made of people, and people are human beings, and human beings care. When you care enough to deliver value to the company, when you honestly care about other people, when you care about the company's goals, and when you try to do everything you possibly can to make the company more successful, the people at the company will notice and they will care back.

If you work for a company right now and you are not sure how to cultivate that passion and excitement, there are three things you can do: borrow inspiration from your colleagues, fall in love with the industry, or figure out how to leverage your current role to gain valuable experience.

Start by talking to other employees at the company, especially people who seem to love what they do or have been there for a while and moved up the ladder. Anyone who is making an impact at the company would probably be a good candidate. Don't underestimate how other people's excitement could get you inspired.

If you have the opportunity, I highly recommend that you talk to the CEO or someone on the executive team. Someone who is directly responsible for success or failure and has an actual stake in the company could get you hooked as well.

If you can't find inspiration through the people around you, I would question whether or not that is a company you want to continue working for. Seriously. If no one around you cares enough about the company, I am not sure it has a bright future.

Let's say you found some inspiration but what worked for your colleague and got them excited doesn't necessarily get you excited. The next step would be to do some research to try and learn more about the market or the industry you are in. Maybe you're not obsessed with your company's product, but if you can find interest in the market and see its potential, it might give you some motivation.

A few years ago, I worked for a Fintech startup where I had to get excited about blockchain. Now, depending on when you're reading this, blockchain technology may be the source of all evil or the sophisticated technological solution for the world's biggest problems. When I had to learn about blockchain, it was controversial, to say the least. I was not a fan, but I had to figure out how to fall in love with it, because my company was using the technology. At the time, the conversation revolved around using blockchain technology to create cryptocurrencies.

I'm sure there's real merit behind the use of decentralized, unregulated currencies. I understood the benefits, but the way it was used in the real world was kind of shady. Cryptocurrencies were used to buy drugs and weapons and do illegal things because they were untraceable. How can you get excited about something like that?

I had to find something good, something that made sense to me, something that I could believe in, so I started digging. I started following influencers in the blockchain community on different social media channels. I started reading blog posts about blockchain technology and how it might help bring more equality to the financial markets. I learned that the ideology behind blockchain was pretty cool. By allowing digital information to be distributed and decentralized (meaning no one owns it) but not copied, blockchain technology was creating the backbone of a new type of Internet. That was something I could get excited about. Who doesn't want a new and cool Internet?

I started reading more and more, looking for all the good things blockchain was enabling, instead of focusing on the few bad players and how they were misusing the technology to make a profit. You can do the same thing. Spend time researching your industry. Get educated about the possibilities and where the market is heading. Spend time engaging with influencers, to gain a new perspective. You may end up finding something you like.

If your company's industry is not getting you excited, and if you can't find inspiration with your colleagues or team members, there's one more thing you can try. You can focus on your career and how that specific company, industry, or role is going to help you get the experience you need to get to your next job. Maybe your role could serve as a stepping stone, in terms of seniority. Maybe it could give you industry or category experience that would set you up for success later on.

If you are not sure how working for that company will help with your career, here is an exercise that can help:

Imagine that you are about to leave your current company for the job of your dreams and you need to update your resume. What are the skills and achievements you need to have under your current role that will make you qualify for your next job? What can you do, to start gaining those skills? What responsibility can you take on, to start piling up the achievements you need?

After spending two years working with startups at Microsoft, I caught the entrepreneurial bug. I wanted to join an early-stage company. In order to lead marketing for a small company, I realized that I would need a different type of marketing experience than the one I gained while working for one of the biggest companies in the world. I needed more hands-on startup experience and I had to figure out how to get it.

Startups were my target audience, and I had access to many of them through the program I was working on. All I had to do was figure out how I could deliver value to those startups while gaining experience and serving Microsoft's interests.

My solution was to volunteer as a startup mentor. I offered office hours for startups where I would help them develop their value proposition, create a marketing strategy, and hire their first marketers. This approach allowed me to learn about the marketing challenges of early-stage companies while keeping my work true to Microsoft's objectives—help startups grow and scale (while using Microsoft's tools and products).

Becoming a mentor was not part of my job description. No one told me I had to do it. I actually had to sell the idea to my manager, because it required a few hours of my time every week. It was my creative solution to the problem I was facing: I didn't have enough relevant experience to qualify for my next role and I wanted to use my time at Microsoft to gain that experience.

If you can't care about the company, care about your career. Use your future as motivation to do more and drive success for the company you work for. After all, the company's success will be reflected on your resume.

When it comes to finding purpose at work, you should know a caveat to everything I just told you. You can't fake it. You actually have to care. You need to get excited about the company and what it is doing. You need to take an interest in the industry, to the extent of learning everything you can about it because you actually want to know. You need to care whether or not your company is successful—not just whether or not you're successful in your role. Otherwise, it will not work.

I don't know what about you, but I don't like waking up in the morning, dreading going to work. I don't want to hate my job; I want to love it. We spend almost half of our day at work, and I want to make sure I spend that time doing something that I truly enjoy doing. I want my job to give me energy, not take it away.

Sometimes, you don't have the privilege of choosing where to work, you just need a job. I understand that you can't just get up and leave the position you're in. However, in the long term, you *can* make choices that support the notion of working only for companies that you care about. Even if you can't change your position today, you can start thinking about a better future and optimizing your actions towards it. Plus, in the meantime, you can take additional steps, to try and fall in love with what you're currently doing.

Think and Act Like an Owner

Now that you have a sense of purpose at work, it's time to dive deeper into what it means to have an owner mentality and how you can start cultivating that habit. Once you start thinking like an owner, it will become your default state, and it won't require too much effort. It will become the lens through which you see everything. However, like any habit, getting there requires some deliberate practice.

You can start right now. There are three pillars that will help you in developing an owner mindset: know the business, do more with less, and go beyond your job description.

1: Know the Business

What does it actually mean to be invested in the company you work for? It starts with understanding how the business works.

No matter what your role is, at the end of the day, your work is meant to drive the company forward and help generate revenue. Even if you are just getting started and it feels like you are a small cog in a big machine, you have to look outside of your own role and see the bigger picture. Whether you are in marketing, sales, finance, or operations, and/or whether you are building the product or sustaining the culture, you need to know the business.

In order to develop an owner mentality, you need to understand how your company makes money and what success looks like.

There are different ways to learn about the company. The easiest and probably the most overlooked way is simply to ask. Ask your manager, your team, the executive team, or the CEO—if you feel comfortable reaching out to them. If you prefer to learn quietly, do some research. Google your company's name and read the articles that come up. The most useful content will probably be stories about funding rounds, analyst reviews, and product updates. You should also explore your company's website and learn about their pricing tiers and their value proposition. Read customer reviews to learn how their product is being used. If you work for a public company, read the quarterly or yearly reports and listen in on earning calls.

If your company sells multiple products, focus on your business unit and how it generates revenue for the company. Learn what the different teams at your company do, to figure out how everything comes together. You can ask guiding questions, such as: Who are our main customers? What is the product or service we offer them? How is it solving a problem? What is our business model? How are we paid and how much are we charging? How much is the company hoping to grow by, this year? Where is this growth going to come from? How are we going to acquire customers?

You don't need to become an expert, you just need to have an understanding of how the business works, so you can see the big picture and how your work contributes to its overall success. Understanding the business will also help you identify opportunities for improvement and growth, even when they are not directly tied to your role.

2: Do More with Less

This is probably one of the biggest differentiators between having an employee mindset versus an owner mindset.

When you work for a company, a budget is an invisible resource (money you don't see) that is given to you, whenever you need it. It's a bit like getting your weekly allowance from your parents when you were a child. Most employees expect the company to provide them and their team with a budget, but they don't spend too much time wondering where it's coming from or how to create more of it.

When you have an owner mindset, you think differently. You feel like the budget is your own money, so you are more careful about how much of it you spend and how you use it. When it feels like you are spending your own money, you want to get the most out of every dollar and avoid throwing any of it away. As a result, you start evaluating your initiatives and expenses quite differently. You focus on generating a return on your investment (ROI) instead of simply doing things for the sake of doing them. You justify spending money with your ability to bring in revenue.

You also spend more time evaluating vendors and service providers. In the past, you may have settled for "good enough" or opted to use the most popular provider, but now you want to make sure you choose partners who have your company's best interests in mind. If you are paying for a service, you want to make sure you get your money's worth.

How can you do more with less? Most people will assume having less money or working with a smaller budget is a disadvantage that is going to keep them from achieving their goals. I'm here to tell you it is exactly the opposite. When you have less, you have to become creative. That's when a person's genius shines through and the best ideas come to life.

When I was consulting for a team at Google, we were looking for ways to grow our reach with our target audience by getting more eyeballs on the content in our blog. At the time, we didn't have dedicated social media channels, so we had to find different ways to promote the content and raise that awareness. We had to show results fast, too, so we couldn't wait for our community to grow. That is where the mindset of doing more with less came in handy.

Instead of focusing on what we didn't have, we focused on the resources that were available to us.

Our blog featured stories and guidelines on how to apply machine learning to tech products—highly technical content, written by experts and practitioners. One of those experts was a well-known author and thought leader in the tech industry. He had quite a following on social media, which gave us an idea. Instead of creating our own distribution channels, what if we use that expert's social media profiles to promote the blog? After all, his followers were part of our audience, he was already contributing by creating the content, and becoming our spokesperson could help him grow his personal brand.

All it took was an iPhone and a one-minute script that summarized the content, for him to help us create a promotional video for every blog post. We shared the video on the expert's LinkedIn profile and linked back to our blog. It was a massive success. With almost zero costs, we were able to generate hundreds of thousands of views for our blog.

We could have spent the majority of our budget on advertising, in order to get people to visit our blog, but we got better results faster by thinking like owners and focusing on doing more with less.

All you need to do to apply this way of thinking is to pretend you don't have a budget and imagine you don't have the headcount or the amount of time it would "normally" take to get the job done. Try to solve your problem with such constraints and help your brain find alternative solutions.

3: Go Beyond Your Job Description

Like rules, job descriptions are meant to be broken, or in this case, expanded.

I know the idea of doing more than what you are paid to do can seem baffling, but it is one of the most effective ways to become invaluable. Typical employees do their job. Invaluable employees go the extra mile. It's not about showing off or being a kiss-ass; it's about delivering value to the company by expanding the limits of what you are supposed to do.

Early in my career, when I worked for a travel agency, my job was to book flights and accommodations for business travelers—you know, spoiled corporate employees who spent more time on airplanes than in the office. I had to endure complaints like "I didn't like the food on the plane" and "How could you book a hotel that doesn't have a gym?" I even heard "I missed my connecting flight because I fell asleep in the business lounge" (true story). Sometimes the customers were rude and sometimes they were annoying, but the travel agency I worked for was known for its superb customer service, and I cared enough to make it my mission to provide the best possible service, in keeping with their tradition.

I remember one time when something went horribly wrong with the travel arrangement made for a senior executive. I messed up his hotel booking during an important conference when the city was booked solid. This was way before Airbnb was an option, and it was bad. I forgot to double-check the reservation and the hotel canceled the booking. I screwed up his trip, and that guy was the complaining type. He called my manager and wouldn't stop yelling about how unprofessional we were and how upset he was.

That screaming session lasted for a while and made me feel really bad. I was devastated, but I knew that he was an important client, so I couldn't afford to sulk. Instead of making excuses or blaming him for reporting my mistake, I decided to do something different. I decided to do what would be in the best interests of the company:

INVALUABLE

I decided to both apologize in person and to compensate him for the inconvenience.

It was Valentine's Day when he got back from his business trip, so I decided to send over flowers and a voucher for a nice breakfast in a fancy restaurant. I found out his office was just a few blocks from mine, so I picked up the flowers and the voucher, added a handwritten apology, and went to his office, to deliver it in person.

I will never forget the look on his face when I explained who I was. He did not know how to react. He kept opening and closing his mouth but he didn't make a sound. He took the flowers and the voucher, he read my apology, and then he asked me to sit down. We had a nice conversation where he told me about the terrible week that he had and that he didn't mean to yell at my boss. He repeatedly mentioned how much he appreciated my gesture and that he would let my manager know he was no longer upset with my service.

I know my approach to this situation was a bit unconventional. It was above and beyond what you would expect, but I couldn't bear the thought of someone thinking we provided bad service. I had to protect my professional reputation as well as the company's. And I did.

Do you want to know what the really cool thing was? That guy was a senior executive at a very big company that was working with two travel agencies, at the time, to evaluate which one should handle the company's travel budget. Guess who won that contract? Of course, we did. He was the guy making the decision, and he chose the company that made a mistake but owned up to it and cared enough to fix it.

There are many ways to go beyond your job description, in order to make an impact. The guiding principle I use to decide if I should go the extra mile is asking myself "Will this help the company?" I also ask myself "If I were the owner or the CEO, would I want my employee to do this?"

Adopting an owner's mindset is all about changing your mindset and the way you think. The more you practice asking yourself the right questions, and trying to see the world from an owner's perspective, the more you will see every situation from two different angles—your own and the company's. Mastering the ability to navigate between the everyday details and the 10,000-foot view, and optimizing for both, are the first steps to becoming an invaluable employee.

Chapter 1 Checklist and Summary

Test yourself to see if you have an owner's mindset by answering these questions:

- ❏ Do you work from nine to five every weekday or do you live the company's mission and vision, 24/7?
- ❏ Do you focus on the work you have to do this week or do you think about next month and next year?
- ❏ Do you try to make clients happy or do you do everything humanly possible to delight them because you know the company depends on it?
- ❏ Do you work on what's urgent or on what is really important and can provide high leverage?
- ❏ Do you adjust to fit the company's culture or do you define the culture, through your actions?
- ❏ Are you reactive or proactive?
- ❏ Do you stick to a tried-and-true approach or do you find new ways to do things?
- ❏ Do you try until you fail or do you refuse to accept that failure is not an option?

How to find your purpose at work:

- ❏ Choose the company you work for
- ❏ Look to your colleagues for inspiration
- ❏ Fall in love with the industry
- ❏ Use your current job as leverage for the next job

Remember the cycle of passion at work:

- ✓ Find meaning or purpose
- ✓ Take small actions to validate your purpose and generate small wins
- ✓ Success = a hit of dopamine that makes you a bit happier
- ✓ Take bigger actions
- ✓ Repeat the cycle

Actionable steps to help you develop an owner's mindset:

1. Know the business
2. Do more with less
3. Go beyond your job description

INVALUABLE

Chapter 2
Skill #2—Become a Lifelong Learner

Right around the time I joined Microsoft, another employee was taking his first steps in a new role. Just six months prior to my arrival, Satya Nadella became Microsoft's CEO. It was both an exciting and confusing time for the company, as everything was changing, but as we all learned a few years later, those changes resulted in great success.

Although it took another year for me to meet Satya in person, I remember the first time I came across his unique approach to learning, called The Growth Mindset program. It was in an interview that was published in one of the top tech blogs in which Satya described a unique and interesting approach he was planning on implementing at Microsoft. It was based on a book by Dr. Carol S. Dweck called *Mindset: The New Psychology of Success*. I wasn't much of a reader at the time, but Satya kept going on and on about how this book changed his life, so I thought I would give it a try—you know, in solidarity to the new CEO and my new role.

In a nutshell, a growth mindset means you view intelligence and the human potential as endless; you

believe people are always able to learn new skills, grow, and improve. In contrast, a fixed mindset means you believe learning is something you're either good at or you're not. You also believe people's traits are fixed, so if someone wasn't born with a specific talent, they'll never have it.

I believe in the former. I know that we can learn, grow, improve, and constantly reinvent ourselves, because I have seen it again and again. The people who put in the time and effort to expand their knowledge are the ones who become a better version of themselves. They advance their career, they are more fulfilled, and they end up doing what everyone else thought was impossible.

When I applied for the social media role at Blonde 2.0, I had almost no experience managing social media channels. What I had was about 100 hours of reading and learning.

Once I realized how far I was able to go just by learning, there was no stopping me. I would start my day with an hour of reading every tech blog in the industry. If anything happened in the social media industry in the previous 24 hours, I knew about it. If there was a new tool, a new startup, or an emerging social media platform, I knew about it.

Being completely plugged in to an up-and-coming industry provided me with a massive competitive advantage. Having all this knowledge and then having the opportunity to use it helped me become invaluable to the company. In four years, I went from being a junior account manager to a supervisor to the team lead to director. I went from being an individual contributor to managing a team of 25 people.

Why Learning is the Most Important Skill You Will Ever Develop

I was able to move up the ladder almost every time I took on a new role. As great as it was from a career perspective, it also meant it was necessary for me to learn new skills and gain experience I didn't have in order to take on those new opportunities.

When you are not 100% qualified for the role you are getting into, you need to spend more time ramping up. You also have to learn fast, to make up for what you are lacking in experience.

Yes, you could stay in your comfort zone and take a job you know exactly how to do. You could save yourself the trouble of having to do so much extra work, but let me tell you a secret. If you are 100% ready for your role, you are looking at the wrong opportunity. If there's no room to grow and learn, why would you want to take that job?

One of the biggest perks that comes with a new job is the possibility of learning and growing. I encourage you to always look for opportunities that are a little bit out of your comfort zone. Look for roles where you have most of the basic knowledge that is required, but where your instincts and your ability to learn quickly could make up for the rest. When you find a role that requires you to be more than who you are right now and you live up to the challenge, you become a better version of yourself. For me, that's a good enough reason to take the more challenging path.

Learning is not the easiest skill to adopt but it can give you a competitive edge in the workplace, and perhaps even in life. The ability to motivate yourself and develop the curiosity (or discipline) that can keep you learning all the time is quickly becoming one of the most important skills in the job market.

Once you internalize that anything can be learned, your mind becomes limitless. You start seeing possibilities, instead of limitations. You become more resilient and less likely to give up. People tend to persist through challenges when they understand that intelligence is malleable, rather than a fixed trait. By becoming a lifelong learner, you'll make it easier for yourself to adopt soft skills and increase your potential for becoming an invaluable employee.

How to Turn Learning into a Habit and Develop a Personal Growth Machine

After a few years with Blonde 2.0, the PR and social media agency, I grew my team to 25 people. If you've been a manager before, you know that having 25 direct reports is an impossible situation. You don't have enough time in the day to solve everyone's problems and do your job well, so I had to be strict when it came to answering questions and giving guidance. Anytime an employee would come to me with a challenge, I would ask them one question before giving them more of my time: "Did you Google it?" As simple and straightforward as this question is, you'd be surprised how many times the answer was "Um... no." Whenever they admitted they hadn't put in the minimum effort of trying to figure it out on their own, I would tell them to turn around, go back to their desks, and try to find the answer on their own first.

I believe we live in a time where people can't really use "I don't know" as an excuse. "I don't know" means "I'm too lazy to Google it," or "I'm not curious enough to make an effort." It means you don't have the right mindset to be invaluable.

Here is a controversial truth: I spent a lot of time and money getting my MBA but the most valuable learnings in my career came through figuring things out on my own by doing a Google search, talking to someone who had more experience than me, or reading (or consulting) a book.

Unfortunately, too many people associate learning with school, so they stay away from anything that reminds them of that time, learning included. They seem to forget that when they were younger, they were eager to learn. We all were.

As children, we have an insatiable curiosity and desire to learn. We want to explore the world and the people around us. However, something happens as we grow older. We experience learning in a negative way, so we stop doing it altogether.

I'm not saying you should pick up biographies or start reading history books about third world problems, if you don't find them interesting. I am saying that if you're into finance, you should learn about the latest tools or regulations in your field. If you're in marketing, you may want to know what the latest tactic is that you can employ to drive more traffic to your website and get qualified leads. If you are in customer support, you may want to know what a standard SLA (service-level agreement) looks like, and if you're managing a team, you should learn about leadership and management strategies. No one is born with all of that knowledge; we all have to learn, in order to become better professionals. You can do the bare minimum and probably get by, or you could embrace learning and become the best in your field.

Like everything else, sticking with learning requires a desire to learn and the tools to turn it into a habit. If you have to convince yourself to learn every single day, you'll get tired quickly and give up. If you want to get to that point where learning becomes a habit, where it's part of your identity and what you do, you need to automate learning. The way to do that is to create a growth machine—a process that constantly delivers the right information to your inbox and social feeds, where you spend most of your time.

Whether you are setting up this growth machine to learn about a new industry or to keep up with your profession, the procedure is quite similar. The goal is to automate your learning process, so it is easier and less time-consuming.

The first step is to get curious. This is probably why it is so important to have a real interest in the companies you work for (or want to work for). Knowing that you are going to have to learn a lot about an industry and a product means you are going to spend hours, days, or weeks learning, so you want to make darn sure you will enjoy it.

Once you have everything in place for the growth machine, and the information starts flowing, you'll be able to turn learning into habit. It may be challenging at the beginning, but the more you do it, the better you'll get at sticking to learning. When you start seeing the benefits and reaping the rewards, it will incentivize you to continue.

Set Up Your Growth Machine Using the 5-Circles Methodology

The first step to building a great growth machine is to learn how to search like a pro. That means going beyond typing a simple search query in Google and learning how to use the algorithm to uncover the most valuable information.

Let me tell you about my first 30 days at Microsoft to demonstrate how to do research the right way.

On my first day on the job, my manager left for a three-week vacation.

I was recruited to help build a new marketing role, one that didn't exist before, and all I had to work with was a very general description and my manager's blessing to do what I thought was right. No pressure!

I had no tasks or guidelines and not a lot of clarity about what was expected of me. I could have taken it easy. I could have spent my time "onboarding," which is the corporate euphemism for resting and relaxing, and no one would have blamed me. Instead, I embraced the situation and decided to take on the challenge. I made it my mission to have an action plan ready for my manager by the time he got back from vacation. Ambitious, I know.

On my second day, I walked into the office, sat down in my chair, and stared at my computer screen. I was trying to figure out how to get started. An annoying sensation was making its way from my stomach to my throat and it became hard to breathe. My brain decided to join the celebration, shooting debilitating questions into my head: *How am I going to do this? What do I know about this company and product? There's so much to learn, I'll never make it on time!*

Those thoughts kept running around in my head, making it impossible to concentrate on the mission at hand. I took a deep breath and tried to relax. *You have three weeks to do this. You don't have to figure everything out today!* It wasn't the first time I experienced imposter syndrome, so I knew there was only one way to get over it: just do it.

I looked at my screen with determination and started typing into the Google search box. My research started with a broad and somewhat random query: "Startups." That was a mistake. Very quickly, I found myself clicking my way into a rabbit hole that started with a TED Talk and ended with a makeup tutorial on

YouTube. That was a waste of time, so I decided to be a bit more intentional in my research. I took a step back and laid out all the information I had.

I knew we were operating in the startup ecosystem, and that we were offering startups access to a program that could help them accelerate the growth of their company. With that information in mind, I began writing down questions: What is a startup? What types of startups are there? How do you become an entrepreneur? Why do entrepreneurs apply for an accelerator program? What are the best accelerator programs in the world? I probably wrote down a dozen more.

One by one, I typed those questions into the Google search bar and followed some of the links to see what the most common answers were. I then copied the best answers into a file with each of the questions, trying to add new information with every article I read. When it seemed like the information was just repeating itself, I'd stop.

I then went back and edited the different clippings, so that they formed a coherent answer.

After working on a few questions, I got the hang of it and was able to skim through articles quickly, picking up only new information.

After a while, I started seeing contextual content suggestions that provided me with additional insights. It answered questions I didn't think about. That was where the real learning started! For example, I knew that venture capitalists were investors who funded startups but I had never heard of CVC before, but Google introduced me to Corporate Venture Capital funds—major players in the startup ecosystem.

At the end of the research process, I had about 20 pages of relevant information that provided me with a basic but solid understanding of the startup and accelerator landscape.

Asking the right questions is key to making your research effective. However, you often won't know enough to ask the right questions, so when you are brand-new to an industry or discipline, look for contextual suggestions from Google to help you get started. But online research will only get you so far, so the next step in your research is to talk to someone with the experience and knowledge you are lacking—a colleague in the company or someone who is an industry expert.

I spent a big portion of my first three weeks talking to my team members and learning from their experience. I wasn't sure what to ask at first, because I didn't know what would be valuable, so I stuck to listening and I let them do most of the talking.

When you listen, pick up cues and focus on uncovering "unknowns." From my experience, when people talk about a topic they know well, they tend to name-drop and use acronyms. It can be confusing, if you are just learning the ropes, so don't be afraid to ask for clarifications. Those little nuggets of information are exactly what you are looking for.

I know, I know. This advice of asking and listening sounds great in theory, but you probably still have some concerns. After all, you just started a new job and you don't want to look like a noob. I totally get it. That is why you should only reach out to peers and experts *after* you did some basic research like browsing through your company's website and the top publication in your industry. You need to put in some effort to learn on your own before reaching out to others, and showing up with some context will help you navigate the conversation. And don't worry, most people will be happy to answer your questions, because most people like hearing themselves speak. I don't know a lot of people who wouldn't enjoy a friendly pat on their ego.

Learning, especially in the professional world, is an ongoing process. Even after all that research, I barely started scratching the surface when it came to the startup ecosystem. No matter how much time you spend doing research early on, you'll need to continue learning as you go, or risk staying behind. You can't expect the industry to stand still or stop evolving, so you need to have a process in place to keep you up-to-date.

This is where I will help you, with my no-fail system, which I have been cultivating for years: the 5 Circles Methodology. By leveraging these five channels, you will be able to get the most relevant information, right at your fingertips. The process will require some time to set up and optimize but once you have it up and running, you will have the ultimate growth machine.

Circle 1: Capture News and Real-Time Updates

The first step in the methodology requires that you set up Google Alerts to capture news and timely updates. You can set alerts to follow your own company name or your competitor's, you can use it to track a specific topic or discipline, and you can even focus on relevant keywords. You want to have 3-5 alerts that capture enough information but not too much. For example, I wouldn't use "startups" because it's too broad of a search. Using "startup accelerator" and even "corporate accelerator" worked well for me, during my time at Microsoft. I suggest trying a few alerts and optimizing as you go. You can always remove the ones that don't provide you with the best results.

You can set your alerts to come in as they happen, or you can choose to have them sent daily or weekly. I recommend the latter. You probably don't want to get 20 emails every day from Google. You don't need any additional stress. There are a few other tools that will allow you to capture real-time news, so feel free to use what works for you. I don't recommend using mobile push notifications because if you get an alert every time one of your searches is updated, you will spend most of your day on your phone.

In addition to real-time updates, you can work on optimizing your social media feed. You can follow company accounts (your company's competitors), news outlets that are relevant to your industry, or simply add specific topics to your feed. With most social media channels today, you can follow a hashtag or topic so the most popular content on that topic shows up in your feed.

Circle 2: Curate, Prioritize, and Automate

In order to have the most relevant and valuable content come to you, you first need to identify the most valuable resources, such as websites, newsletters, and podcasts that share the type of knowledge you are looking to acquire. Start by mapping out the main publications, blogs, and company websites in your industry. Make a list of these sources and try to evaluate which ones will be the most relevant for you, then rank them according to their relevance. You want to end up with a list of 10 sources of information that are specific to your industry or to the topic you are trying to learn. When I was at Microsoft, publications like TechCrunch, VentureBeat, and entrepreneur.com were some of the obvious resources. When I wanted to learn more about marketing in the SaaS B2B industry, the SaaStr podcast, and Intercom's blog were a couple of my main resources.

Finding the right resources may require some trial and error. The best way to test out which ones work is to sign up for email updates on all of them and then check if you regularly open their updates. If you end up deleting their emails before you even open them, then unsubscribe. The idea behind this process is to help you narrow down the amount of information you get in your inbox. You want to focus only on what is valuable for you.

Every time I add a topic to my growth machine or enter a new industry, I start with a lot of newsletters. After a few weeks, it becomes clear which ones I'm actually reading. The majority of the work happens at the beginning, when you spend time identifying the best resources.

Note that this is an ongoing process.

The more you learn, the more you will be exposed to new resources. That means you will constantly add newsletter subscriptions you discover as you go. Some of the old ones may become obsolete and you will remove them.

In order to make the most out of the content I get in my inbox, I try to maintain a reference list. If I come across a great piece of content that I want to save for later, I add it to a "read it later" app like Pocket or save it to a file on my Google Drive. By curating this content, I'm creating a private library of blog posts, e-books, and templates that I can use whenever I need or want to.

By creating an automated flow of information, you are making learning inevitable. When something is sitting in your inbox staring at you, you are more likely to acknowledge it and use it, which makes it a hundred times easier for you to turn learning into a habit.

Circle 3: Create and Commit to a Reading List

Books are one of the best sources you can use to expand your knowledge on a specific topic. Reading professional nonfiction books requires a bigger investment of your time, but it is usually worth it. Books, such as the one you are reading now, are very often based on years of experience. They contain valuable knowledge as well as excellent, actionable strategies (usually gained through trial and error), which have been proven to work.

More often than not, professional books were written by people who've successfully done what you are trying to do, and figured out how to do it well. Those people used their experience, created methodologies and techniques that could make your life easier, and shared their expertise in their books.

By reading a book, you can condense years of learning into one weekend. That is a very efficient way to go deeper into a specific topic. The sad truth is that about 50% of people never read a book after they graduate from high school, and out of those who read, even fewer read non-fiction and professional literature. Since you are reading this book, you understand how valuable books are and that they can serve as virtual mentors, channeling the thoughts and ideas of experts, through their pages.

Having said that, I know it's hard to keep up this habit and commit to reading, so I'm going to share a little secret with you. Up until around 2013, I didn't read books—at all. The thought of picking up a biography or a professional book was mind-boggling. Then something strange happened and completely changed my perspective. It was around the time my husband and I started dating. During one of the first times I stayed at his place overnight, I couldn't sleep. I was up at the crack of dawn while he slept like a baby, so I got up and started walking around his tiny apartment, looking for something to do that would keep me busy and wouldn't wake up the sleeping beauty. After walking back and forth across the apartment several times, I ended up in front of a small bookcase. It had about 30 books in it, all perfectly organized by size (this is how I knew we were soulmates!). I started reading the titles hoping to find something I liked. All of his books were about peak performance, building a business, and developing skills. What a drag. I turned around and sat on the sofa for a few minutes, hoping for something to happen. No luck. It was 7 AM on a Sunday and the world was still asleep. Realizing I probably wouldn't have a better option, I went back to the bookcase and decided to pick the shortest book I could find. It was called *Naked Economics*, by Charles Wheelan. I majored in economics and I kind of hated it, but this was an emergency, so I decided to give it a shot.

About two hours later, when my gracious host finally woke up, I was so caught up with reading the book that I didn't notice time had flown by. I was halfway through the book. I couldn't believe it—I was fascinated by economics.

As it turned out, I had chosen one of the best books ever written about the subject, but instead of it being more like a textbook, which is what I expected, it was borderline stand-up comedy. The stories included everyday examples that made the book fun to read. I kid you not, I even found myself giggling every now and then. That was a turning point for me. Once I realized that not all nonfiction books were boring, I was willing to try and read a few more.

Reading books requires a bigger commitment of your time so you need to find a way to remove any and all obstacles, starting with the burden of making a choice. Deciding which books to read can be a daunting task. It requires research, comparisons, and tradeoffs. If every time you decide to read a book, you'll have to go through all of these emotionally draining tasks, you will never read a book. You will be too worn out with decision fatigue to even consider it, which is no good, so here is what you can do instead: you can create a reading list that will last for a while.

There are five easy parts to the circle of creating and committing to a reading list.

First, start by mapping out a few books that may help you in your career. If you are not sure what you might like, use Amazon.com, book recommendation websites like BookAuthority.org, or just ask your friends and/or colleagues for their favorite business books. You should be able to find at least five books to put on your list.

Second, choose two books out of your list and buy them. Don't think about it. Just do it. Buying the books, even if you buy digital copies or audio versions, tells your brain that you are making a commitment. You feel obligated to follow through because you already took action.

Third, begin reading. Hopefully, you are a little bit excited to get started, so give yourself the opportunity to dive right in. Start reading immediately, even if you only get through a few pages.

Fourth, if you update your list every now and then, you will always have a go-to book, and you won't get stuck. I now have a good list of books that I curated over the years, based on recommendations from the influencers I follow and the articles I read.

Fifth, set up a goal for how many books you want to read over a period of time. This is a good way to help you avoid procrastination. When I decided I wanted to start reading nonfiction books, I challenged myself to read one book every month. I know it sounds like a lot. It sounded impossible to me at the time, considering the only book I read was *Fifty Shades of Grey* the previous year, but I had a secret weapon: a strong sense of accountability. I never break a promise I make to myself. It's embedded in my identity to be the person who follows through.

So, when I set up a challenge for myself, I don't let myself down. If you don't have that sense of accountability yet, you can make your commitment public. Tell your family, your friends, and/or share it on social media. Do whatever it takes to make yourself follow through with your commitment. Your commitment doesn't have to be one book every month. Maybe you will promise yourself you'll read two books this year. Do whatever works for you. The point is to set up a goal, otherwise you'll end up with a wish list, not a reading list.

Circle 4: Follow and Engage with Influencers

The first thing I do every time I jump into a new industry is follow the Influencers, experts, and thought leaders in that ecosystem. Whether it's on social media, their YouTube channel, or a podcast, I identify the trend-setters and listen to what they have to say. It keeps me up to date, but it also makes me feel like part of an insider community.

If you did your industry research well, it's almost guaranteed that you came across a few names already. Those influencers are usually the ones who are creating the most interesting content for your industry or profession, so it's quite likely that you will have stumbled on something they wrote or said.

If that's not the case, you can simply search Google for "top influencers" or "top experts" in your industry. You could also do a search for the most relevant hashtags in your industry on platforms like LinkedIn and Twitter. Browse through the content and find posts that have a lot of engagement. Those posts were most likely written by the people you are looking for.

Once you find your influencers, follow them on the platform that you use the most. It will make it easier for you if you see them in the feed that you browse daily. To make it even easier, I focus on one or two platforms—in my case, LinkedIn and Instagram—and follow all of the influencers on the same platform. It will save you time and help you engage, if you constantly see valuable content on your feed. Think of it as your daily dose of knowledge.

Following thought leaders is a great start, but nothing beats having a real conversation. As scary as it may sound, reach out and engage with those influencers. Whether you need to learn more about a new industry or just ask about their career path, speaking with people who have achieved what you are trying to achieve is another great way to uncover unknown unknowns.

Also, pursue opportunities to meet those people, because one conversation with them could end up being more valuable than reading a hundred of their posts. Those influencers are probably super-connectors in your industry. They will be able to recommend the best vendors, help you find great talent (if you are hiring), and they will be able to refer you to the next influencer you want to talk to. Last but not least, they may be able to help you find your next career opportunity when you start looking for one.

I know what you might be thinking: *Maya, this idea sounds great, but why would any of these people want to talk to me? What do I have to offer? They have celebrity status and insanely busy lives!*

You are right. The experts you want to talk to are usually busy professionals, but they are also just regular people who want to give back. Why else would they be sharing their content?

Invaluable employees want to be the best at what they do so badly that they look past that limiting belief. As long as you do it thoughtfully and tactfully, I can almost guarantee you'll get a "yes."

Here is how I know.

My husband proposed to me on my birthday, and a month-and-a-half later, we got married in a beautiful ceremony. This short schedule didn't leave much time for me to come up with an idea for the perfect wedding gift. I wracked my brain to find a thoughtful way to show him how excited I was to start our life together. Two-and-a-half weeks before the wedding, I found it.

My husband has good taste. His role models include bestselling authors, industry icons, and successful entrepreneurs—people who touch tens of thousands of lives every day and lead successful and busy lives.

I decided to reach out to the influencers who have been a source of inspiration for my husband, and ask them to give us their advice for a happy marriage, for a video compilation I wanted to make for him. I couldn't imagine why they would want to talk to me; I was a stranger they had never met, and I was asking them for a pretty big favor. Luckily, I was running out of time, so I had no choice but to try. Procrastination and doubt were not going to help me put a smile on my husband's face.

Use a Simple Formula

I used a simple formula that works every time, in every context, which you can use, too.

You only need to remember three things: **write like you talk, make it personal, and make it easy for them to help you.**

Let's dig into these three, because too many people get it wrong.

"Write like you talk" means exactly what you think it means—use a casual tone with no formalities. You want to keep it light-hearted and friendly.

When I say "make it personal," I'm not asking you to pour your heart or share a sob story. In general, making it personal is not about you and what you want, it's about them. It's about showing appreciation, it's about leading with recognition, and it's about showing them you took the time to get to know them. I rarely send out a message to a role model without doing the research that is required to learn more about them and what they care about. You can call it online stalking (technically, that's what you will be doing), but I prefer to look at it as the prep work required to build a strong pitch. I like to go through the last few posts they shared on social media, read blog posts they wrote, watch videos they created, and listen to podcast interviews they did. Just by listening to one episode, you can learn about your influencer's career and their philosophy. More often than not, you can also get a glimpse into their "real" life.

With this information in mind, craft a pitch that shows you appreciate them—without sucking up. I can't emphasize that enough. No ass-kissing! That's not the goal of this approach. What you can do is reference something you learned from them, mention something they said that resonated with you, or comment on an observation they have made. Be honest and share your real feedback; don't just say what you think people want to hear.

Keep in mind that influencers and experts are usually successful people. They have busy lives with many commitments and not enough time in the day. That means they have to get really good at making quick decisions when it comes to their precious time. Making it easy for them to quickly say "yes" is the best way to get what you want. The way to do that is to be direct and say exactly what you want. Get to the point quickly and clearly explain what you need from them. Don't lay out your entire life story only to get to your point in the third paragraph. Instead, use the formula I use.

Introduce yourself briefly (for context), show appreciation, and use one sentence to explain why you are reaching out to them. Then, make your "ask." Don't beat around the bush, don't give them options, and don't leave it up to them to suggest a meeting. You need to make it easy for them to understand and to respond quickly.

Here is what a LinkedIn note from me might look like:

Hi [influencer's name], I really enjoyed your latest interview on the SaaStr podcast. As a marketer who grew from Director to VP (Vice President) at the same company, I could relate to the challenges you experienced, especially with hiring the wrong people. I'm actually working through some leadership challenges right now, as I am growing as an executive, and I was hoping to get your advice. Would you be open to jumping on a quick call to discuss this? I'd be happy to accommodate your schedule and grab 30 minutes whenever you are available. Thanks!

By explaining exactly what you want (advice about how to face challenges in my role as an executive), defining a time frame (30 minutes), and a method (a phone call), you make the decision easier. They don't have to fill in the blanks and make assumptions about what you want. They don't need to wonder whether they will enjoy the conversation or if it will be a complete waste of time, and they don't need to give up anything else in order to meet you, because you are telling them you will work around their schedule.

If you send an email and not a LinkedIn message, you may want to introduce yourself, to add some context.

I have used this method over and over again and it works. You will never get a hundred percent response rate—some people say no and others never respond—but in many cases, the answer will be a "yes."

I ended up hearing back from most of the influencers I reached out to for my wedding video. Although some wrote back to say they couldn't help, I still got their attention. None of those influencers knew me or had a reason to help me out, and yet they did. They took time out of their crazy busy days because I asked them for a favor. If I could get them to record a video for my wedding, you can easily get a meeting or a phone call.

The wedding video featured Professor Dan Ariely, a renowned Behavioral Economics researcher and a bestselling author; David Allen, the GTD® (Getting Things Done®) time management method creator and bestselling author; Gary Vaynerchuk, author, entrepreneur, and social media guru; and more. I will never forget the look on my husband's face when he saw some of his virtual mentors look at the camera and talk to him directly, congratulating him on his wedding day. It's one of those priceless memories you carry with you forever.

Circle 5: Join a Community

From attending meetups and events to joining professional groups and online channels, being part of a community with a shared interest and engaging with people you can easily talk to and learn from is quite empowering. It becomes even better when you reach a point where you can help others and share your experience and knowledge with the community.

Some people thrive when they are surrounded by people, so they prefer attending live events. Others are not fans of loud and crowded gatherings, so they opt for the online versions, like joining Facebook, LinkedIn, or Slack groups.

What I like most about these types of interactions is that they usually revolve around one main topic, so the conversation is quite focused and relevant. Many communities host a variety of members, ranging from beginners to veterans, which makes it a safe place for anyone who wants to ask "dumb" questions and get professional advice. I love this circle because it is all about harnessing the wisdom of the crowd to help you learn and win!

This step is a little bit harder to automate, but you can be a lot more intentional when it comes to meeting in group settings. A really good way to constantly be notified about relevant events in your area is to register on an event platform like Meetup or Eventbrite. Choose the most relevant groups and sign up for updates. The event updates will show up in your inbox. If you built the automation part of your growth machine earlier, you will receive event notifications from your favorite influencers and companies as well. You may also learn about discussion groups or Facebook and Slack communities through these email updates you signed up for. (Slack is a business communication platform.)

Join different groups and events—online or offline. Listen or start a conversation. They are usually invaluable resources because they bring together practitioners who share their knowledge on a regular basis.

How to Make the Most out of Your Growth Machine

The growth machine works best when you know what you are optimizing for.

Consider how deep and how wide you need to go on each topic. Sometimes, it's better to have some knowledge about a wide variety of topics to do your job well, and sometimes it's important to go very deep into one specific area. Identify what you need and make sure you're optimizing your learning towards that goal.

You may also want to allocate time on your calendar to read and learn. You'll have plenty of triggers to remind you—that's the whole point of this system—but at least at the beginning, block time on your calendar for learning.

Becoming a lifelong learner is not hard. However, in order to make it a habit and a natural part of your life, you need to make it something you enjoy doing. It is so much easier to spend time in front of the TV than it is to read a book, but in order to become the best version of yourself, you have to continue growing, and that means learning.

My ability to consume content went from 0 to 100 when I started using the growth machine. By creating an automated system that delivers content directly into my inbox or social media feeds, I was able to turn learning into habit. So can you!

One of the things that make invaluable employees stand out is that they constantly reinvent themselves. It means they constantly become better, so they qualify for better jobs. This is why they get promoted faster, this is why they're given more responsibility, and this is why they perform at a higher level than anyone else. The only way to constantly reinvent yourself is to keep learning.

Chapter 2 Checklist and Summary

Learning is the most important skill you will ever develop.
- ❏ Asking the right questions is key to making your research effective.
- ❏ When you listen, pick up cues and discover "unknowns."

Turn learning into a habit.

Develop a personal growth machine, using the 5 Circles Methodology:

1. Capture news and real-time updates
   - ❏ Set up smart Google Alerts
   - ❏ Review your daily email

2. Curate, prioritize, and automate the flow of information
   - ❏ Map out the best resources (blogs, publications, company websites)
   - ❏ Signup for email updates (newsletters)
   - ❏ Test quality and eliminate content that is not valuable, optimizing for 10 resources
   - ❏ Set up time to read content weekly

3. Create and commit to a reading list
    - ❏ Map out a list of books to read (using recommendations sites and Amazon)
    - ❏ Make a commitment to read X number of books every year
    - ❏ Buy 1-2 books
    - ❏ Start reading immediately

4. Follow and engage with influencers
    - ❏ Identify influencers in your industry
    - ❏ Follow them on one main platform, to optimize your feeds
    - ❏ Engage with their content
    - ❏ Reach out and ask for a conversation to learn more

5. Join a community
    - ❏ Map out communities and events (using Meetup, Eventbrite, and/or Slack)
    - ❏ Become an observer and/or an active participant
    - ❏ Connect with community members in real life

INVALUABLE

Chapter 3
Skill #3—Focus on Making an Impact

I can't remember the exact year, but it was sometime in my early 20s, when I was working for the travel agency. What I do remember is how I felt when I opened the box that was in front of me. As I carefully unwrapped the book that was inside, I felt guilty and disappointed in myself.

At age 70, my grandmother decided to take writing classes, which eventually led her to write a memoir that laid out her extraordinary life story—from driving her mother crazy with her amusing pranks as a child, through her military service in Alexandria (where she met my grandfather, who was also serving in the British army), to building one of the first towns in Israel (with her bare hands), all the way to the time she spent volunteering in South Africa, teaching locals how to grow and cook their own food.

Throughout the years, I have heard bits and pieces of these stories, but I never realized how exceptional my grandma was, until I finished reading her book.

I gently closed the cover and there it was, staring at me: my shameful mistake.

You see, what my grandmother cared most about was family. She was so proud of her little tribe that she decided to use a photo of the entire family as the cover for her book. Every single family member was there, smiling and proud. Everyone except for me.

To this day, I regret making the decision not to show up.

I wasn't sick, I wasn't traveling, and I wasn't going to lose my job if I took a day off. Yet, I didn't make it because my priorities were wrong.

At the time, I was obsessed with doing more. I thought working 16-hour days was the only way to be valuable and advance my career. Looking back, I probably spent half of my career focusing on getting things done, as opposed to getting the *right* things done. I got things done, but I was also burned out and wasn't able to maximize my potential. I was operating under the assumption that I had to get *everything* done. No detail was too small. I was obsessed with accomplishing everything on my task list, regardless of how impactful (or not) it was.

That mentality and the actions I took positioned me as "the person who gets shit done," but not necessarily as the most valuable. Even with all that hard work, I wasn't gaining the right reputation to grow my career—and I was paying a personal price for taking too much on. You'd think I would have learned my lesson after missing that photo shoot for my grandmother's book. I didn't.

It was only a few years later that I realized I needed to rethink how I spend my energy. I was working for Microsoft then, leading the product marketing for Microsoft's startup accelerator team. We ran startup programs around the world to support entrepreneurship and drive innovation under Microsoft's brand name and my main goal was to help position Microsoft as a valuable partner for startups.

I knew what my "North Star" looked like, yet I spent weeks on a redundant project to clean and update an old SharePoint library—a shared folder that hadn't been used in almost three years! Every team I worked with at Microsoft had its own internal hub, so I assumed our team needed to have one too.

The process of bringing that folder back to life was long and grueling. I went over every single document to decide whether to keep it, update it, or archive it, to avoid confusion. Now, don't get me wrong, I am all for fixing problems and taking on tasks that are not directly related to your role, *if* they have the potential to deliver a massive impact. Cleaning up that folder did not have that potential. Unfortunately, I was 90% done with that task when I realized that no one cared. Since that folder was idle for so long, the team found new ways to share content and had no interest in going back to using that library.

On the one hand, I was devastated. I felt like such a fool. I had effectively performed a useless task. On the other hand, I had a revelation: **I should only focus on doing things that drive a real impact.** Ta-da!

After spending almost two months organizing that folder, with no results to show for it, I finally realized I need to **focus on outcomes, not outputs**.

Here is why: "There is nothing so useless as doing efficiently that which should not be done at all." I think Peter Drucker was able to sum it beautifully in that quote.

Bingo! Don't do stuff for the sake of doing it! Do things that are use*ful*, not use*less*.

I don't know what about you, but I don't enjoy feeling like I'm wasting my time. I mean, I see myself as a valuable contributor, and I make a difference through my work, so why would I settle for delivering meaningless outputs, when I have a choice?

Think about it. If I would have spent that same amount of time focusing on our North Star goal, I could have generated better outcomes. I would have been able to make 10 times the impact and become a lot more valuable as a professional.

Looking back, I think I knew I was wasting my time, but I was scared to take something off of my task list. I was worried that giving up on a task would mean I was not doing enough. I thought having fewer checked off boxes on my task list would mean I wasn't good at my job.

Obviously I was wrong, but I had to prove it to myself to be sure.

I came up with an experiment to help me validate my assumption. I looked at all of the different tasks I had on my To-Do list and started prioritizing them. My guiding principle was very simple. I asked myself: "Is this going to have an impact that will move me towards my main goal?"

I ended up completely eliminating the bottom 20% of my task list (although I was terrified of dropping the ball). Here's the funny part: nothing bad happened. I am serious. No one even noticed, except for me. Everything I was afraid of was just in my head.

Once I realized the power of this elimination process, I started doing it on a regular basis—not because I wanted to have fewer tasks on my list, but because I wanted to make room for more meaningful tasks. I didn't eliminate tasks because I didn't like doing them or because they were too hard. **I eliminated tasks**

that wouldn't make a difference if they were not carried out.

There's a misconception around work. We have a tendency to think "more is better," but that is not always the case. More often than not, it pays off to do fewer things but to do them *well*.

Your Impactful System

I want to help you develop a system that will allow you to prioritize your tasks and focus on the actions that will deliver the biggest impact. If you follow four simple guidelines, you'll never do useless work again.

1: Make sure that you are "long-term greedy."

I know you might be thinking that being greedy is a bad thing. Maybe you're wondering why I am asking you to think this way. Here's the thing: being "long-term greedy" means you take the bigger picture into account, *in every situation*. When someone is long-term greedy, they prioritize the long-term benefits, instead of looking for instant gratification. It usually means they look beyond what they can get right now and think about what they'll get in a few weeks, in a year, or even in a decade.

By applying the long-term greedy point of view to your decision-making, you'll be able to weed out distractions and focus on doing the most impactful tasks.

When I took on leading a team at Blonde 2.0, I had no management experience. One day, I was an individual contributor (like everyone else), and the next, I was a manager. It was confusing, and initially, I had no idea what to do. I wasn't sure what managers did, so I kept doing my old job and took on additional responsibilities. That was a big mistake—in fact, huge.

Being a good manager meant I had to spend time with every team member, I had to develop processes to streamline the work, and it meant I had to track everything we were doing.

That's a lot of additional responsibility, especially when you inherit five employees from the get-go. It took a few weeks of drowning in work until I realized I had to delegate. I couldn't keep doing everything I was doing before as an individual contributor *and* be a good manager.

The problem was that delegating didn't come easy for me. I was afraid of letting go and trusting someone else to do my job. I also knew that delegating would require training and spending time doing (and redoing) some of the work with my team. It was going to take longer to get the work done, and all I wanted was to deliver results faster. Delegating was a hard decision to make.

On the one hand, I could delegate simple, one-off tasks, and keep doing the impactful work myself. In theory, that was the perfect solution. I could delegate immediately and get some much-needed time back, without spending hours on coaching my team. On the other hand, delegating the most complex aspects of my job could provide more value in the long run. It would help me upskill the team and free up more time for me to focus on being a manager. I was tempted. I knew I had to let go and trust my team to rise to the challenge, even if it meant delivering less than perfect results in the short term. Yet, it was so easy to go for the quick fix.

As I was debating these two options, an even scarier thought made its way into my head: *What if one of my team members ends up outperforming me? What if I teach my employees everything I know, and they end up delivering better results than I ever could? Wouldn't that be embarrassing?*

I would love to tell you that I immediately opted for the long-term solution, but I didn't. I was scared of losing control, so I delegated the mundane tasks. I tried to make that work, but it wasn't sustainable.

The work kept piling on and I was dropping the ball, on all fronts. It was time to be long-term greedy and delegate the real work, even though it was going to be hell for the first few weeks.

Spending hours on training while still doing most of the heavy lifting was not easy. Instead of getting more time to focus on managing, I got less. It was grueling and painful. Eventually, it paid off. Not only did I get the free time I needed, I had a stronger, more capable team that could take on new responsibilities and make a bigger impact.

The way to apply long-term greedy thinking into your work is to take into account the bigger picture and the potential for long-term gains—in every decision and situation, especially when it is hard.

Obviously, some tasks won't have meaningful long-term implications. Some things are time-sensitive or simply too tactical to have a long-term impact. The key here is to develop the habit of asking yourself whether you are being long-term greedy. Whenever you are making a decision, ask yourself: *How will this decision play out now and in the future? If I spend more time and effort right now, will I get better results later? Am I settling for a short-term solution because it's easier?*

2: Use "first-principle thinking" to ask the right questions.

It is so easy to get comfortable and complacent in your work. After all, following instructions and maintaining the status quo doesn't require a lot of brainpower. Don't fall into the trap of doing things the way they have always been done. Complacency is a dangerous mindset that can stop you from optimizing for impact.

Luckily, there is an easy way to make sure you constantly think about creative ways to drive impact. In fact, it is so simple that most people miss it!

All you need to do is ask the right questions.

Let me use an oldie but goodie to explain this one. If your boss asked you to jump would you ask how high, or would you ask why they want you to jump? What I'm suggesting is that you get in the habit of asking *why*. When you figure out the why, if it still makes sense to jump, you can then ask how high.

I first learned about first-principle thinking from Elon Musk. That is how he is able to come up with such unique ideas and make smart decisions that drive billions in revenue for his companies.

In its core, first-principle thinking is the practice of actively questioning every assumption you think you "know," in order to come up with more creative solutions. The goal is to focus on the root cause of problems, so you can make decisions that are based on facts and goals, instead of relying on opinions and so-called "best practices."

When I was consulting for Google, I worked with the marketing team to develop their strategy for the following year. To come up with a valuable plan, I had to audit everything that the team had done prior to my arrival. During one of the planning sessions with the team, I learned their biggest focus in the previous year was creating customer testimonial videos. The team had produced several such videos throughout the year and they assumed they should just continue creating them, because no one told them otherwise.

There was only one problem. My audit clearly showed the videos were not getting any traction. They had a very low view count, which meant they were not helping increase the awareness for the team's program. The videos were not delivering the results the team needed, yet they were still considered a high-priority task.

It was time for me to ask a few more questions, to get to the core of the problem. I needed to know why those videos were not working. Was it because the content wasn't interesting? Was it in the wrong format? Or was it because they weren't promoted to the right audience?

We had to find out what was the real problem, and we had to do it quickly. Unless we could prove those videos were capable of driving awareness, there was no justification to continue working on them.

In order to get results quickly, the team partnered with marketers from other business units at Google—ones who were engaging with the same target audience—to promote the videos on their social media channels. Utilizing existing distribution channels allowed the team to get results quickly! They were able to get the videos in front of potential customers and learn that the videos were simply not hitting home. The team learned it wasn't about their ability to reach a large audience, it was just the wrong content.

That was great news! It meant we could focus on solving the real problem—creating more relevant content—and not waste time on a legacy task that carried over from the previous year.

The team collected feedback from the audience who watched the old videos and learned what they could do differently, to create better content. They only produced one video and tested out their new direction, before making a bigger investment. The results were incredible. Their audience loved the new video, their internal partners were happy to get valuable content, and the team ended up gaining tens of thousands of views—and spreading the word about their program, in the process.

By asking a few questions, the team was able to shift from spending time and money on a task that wasn't making an impact at all to spending less time and money on the right task and achieving successful results.

There are different methods to apply first-principle thinking, but there is one simple tactic you can use anytime. It is called the "5 Whys" technique and it was developed by a Toyota executive who wanted to optimize factory work. All you have to do is ask why, until you can't ask why anymore. Each answer forms the basis of the next question, allowing you to get to the root cause of the problem or the root goal. Sometimes, you don't need to ask why five times. Sometimes, you can get to the root of things using fewer whys. The point of the technique is to simply keep asking why.

If we applied this thinking to the Google video story, this is what it would look like:

Assumption: we need to create testimonial videos.

Why? To capture success stories.

Why? So we can share it with entrepreneurs.

Why? To promote the program and get more entrepreneurs to sign up.

Why? To deliver business results.

Why? To reach revenue goals.

When we went through this process, it became clear that creating testimonial videos was not the goal. It was the solution to a problem: deliver business results.

We then had new questions: Is this the only way to deliver the business results we need? Is there a better way to achieve our goal?

We were not ready to give up on videos as a way to generate awareness, but it was clear something wasn't working. We had to apply the 5 Whys technique again, to find out why they were not gaining traction.

Current situation: the videos are not delivering business results.

Why? Our audience wasn't exposed to them.

Why? We didn't promote them.

Why? We don't have distribution channels.

This line of questioning helped us realize that creating videos wasn't enough. We had to get them in front of the right audience. Armed with this knowledge, we were able to make better decisions for the marketing strategy. Instead of producing *more* videos, we were able to test the existing ones, learn what was not working, produce the *right* videos, get them in front of our target audience, and generate measurable business results. We optimized for impact instead of carrying on with a legacy task, and that made all the difference.

It might require some practice to figure out what to ask, in order to get to the bottom of every challenge, but you can use a few of these questions to guide you:

1) Is this the real problem?
2) What are we trying to achieve?

3) If we are successful, what would happen? What does success look like?
4) What is the outcome we are optimizing for?
5) Is this the best way to get results or is there a different way to solve this problem?

Question everything you know and believe, to get the best results, even if it means you need to question the way things have always been done or what your manager told you to do. By stripping the problem to its bare elements, you'll be able to focus on the real challenge and come up with better solutions that make an impact.

3: Avoid "sunk cost bias."

Imagine you are eating at a fancy restaurant and it seems like you have ordered too much food, but instead of stopping when you are full, you overeat, because you want to get your money's worth. Sound familiar? How about watching a movie all the way through, even though you knew it sucked after the first 30 minutes?

We have the tendency to follow through, just because we made the decision to start doing something. This phenomenon is known as "sunk cost fallacy" or "sunk cost bias," and we all experience it throughout our lives. While wasting an hour on a terrible movie won't have major repercussions, wasting precious time on the wrong project at work can impact the company's success.

When you choose a task or project to focus on, you believe it's the right thing to do. You make a decision based on what you know at that time, and run with it.

Good—that's what you are supposed to do.

The challenge is to go back and reevaluate what you are working on, in order to make sure you are not just following through for the sake of following through.

Even though you don't see it, it is quite possible that you started working on a project that was meaningful at the time, but due to a change of circumstances, it is no longer the best course of action.

It's easy to fall into the sunk cost bias and continue an endeavor just because you have previously invested resources in it like time, effort or money. It's perfectly normal to feel that way. You are human.

We are all wired to try and avoid loss and pain, so we convince ourselves it's better to complete our task than lose what we have invested.

I have yet to find a good way to *completely* avoid sunk cost bias, but there are a few things you can do, to make sure you are not letting it get the better of you.

Develop a system of checks and balances. Simply put, have a process for reviewing ongoing projects and tasks, so you can re-evaluate their impact (and eliminate them, if necessary) before you develop a strong attachment. This isn't something you should do every week, but it could be part of your monthly or quarterly review. Alternatively, prompt yourself to re-evaluate decisions, whenever there's a big change in circumstances (such as a downturn in the economy, a market shift, the development of new technology, emerging trends, or a meaningful change in the results your work is producing). If you are not sure, ask a colleague to share their feedback on the relevance of your work. They have no attachments to what you are working on, so they won't be affected by the sunk cost fallacy and could provide an unbiased opinion.

Consider alternative costs. Every time you say yes to a project, a channel, or a new strategy, you are essentially saying no to all other alternatives—everything else you could have spent your time on. Thinking about those alternatives could help you identify and eliminate sunk cost bias.

You can make sure you consider the alternative costs by asking yourself these questions: *If I were to stop working on this task, what would I be able to do instead? What are the alternatives to this project? What is the result I anticipate for each alternative? Will I be able to make a bigger impact, if I spend my time elsewhere?*

Let go of emotional attachments. We tend to cling to our original decisions, even though we know they are no longer serving us, in an effort to avoid pain. We don't want to admit we were wrong and feel ashamed. The more emotional attachment we have to a project, the harder it is to admit that it won't succeed.

I've seen people make terrible excuses that make no sense and even manipulate results, just to avoid an admission of failure. That is ridiculous. No one gets everything right. If you are alive and working, if you are learning and growing, if you are trying new things and thinking creatively, you will fail. Accept it, embrace it, and move on.

As my husband always tells me: you need to operate with a high intention and a low attachment. Get excited, go all in, and invest in what you are doing—but be skeptical and know that at any given moment, you may need to let go. You may also want to remind yourself that when you stop doing something that isn't producing the results you want, you get time back, to focus on something that can become a massive success.

4: Use a prioritization matrix.

One last tool you can use to make sure all of your projects are geared towards making an impact is a prioritization matrix. When you have to prioritize your work, you are forced to think how to spend your time, to maximize the impact of your work. You have to take into account how each task could move you towards your goals, and compare it with the time and effort you will need to invest in order to complete it.

Depending on your role and your seniority, you may need to face difficult tradeoffs, in order to prioritize your work. I like to keep things simple, so I use a prioritization matrix with four quadrants, to help me label each task. The tasks are based on impact and urgency, where impact is used as the scale on the vertical axis, and urgency is used on the horizontal axis.

Tasks that are urgent and could have a high impact should be prioritized and worked on now. Tasks that are not urgent but have a potential to make an impact should be prioritized as do next. Tasks that are urgent but are not expected to have a big impact should be done last or outsourced, and tasks with no urgency and no clear potential for impact should be eliminated.

There is no "one size fits all" formula for prioritizing. Different products, different industries, and different goals will require different actions to move forward. The key is to understand the framework, so you can apply it to any situation.

Your time is probably the most valuable resource, so you have to use it wisely. The ability to prioritize well is one of the things that separate invaluable employees from their colleagues.

When it comes to making an impact at work, you have a choice. You can be the person who gets things done, or you can be the person who gets the *right* things done. Invaluable employees do the latter.

> **Chapter 3 Checklist and Summary**
>
> To make an impact:
>
> 1. Make sure you are long-term greedy and consider the big picture in every decision
>   - ❏ How will this decision play out now and in the future?
>   - ❏ If I spend more time and effort right now, will I get better results later?
>   - ❏ Am I fixing the problem or just the symptoms?
>
> 2. Use first-principle thinking to ask the right questions
>   - ❏ Use the 5 Whys technique
>
> 3. Avoid sunk cost bias
>   - ❏ Develop a system of checks and balances
>   - ❏ Consider alternative costs
>   - ❏ Let go of emotional attachments

4. Focus on the work that matters, using a prioritization matrix
   - ❑ Tasks that are urgent and could have a high impact should be prioritized and worked on now.
   - ❑ Tasks that are not urgent but have a potential to make an impact should be prioritized as do next.
   - ❑ Tasks that are urgent but are not expected to have a big impact should be done last
   - ❑ Tasks with no urgency and no clear potential for impact should be eliminated

Chapter 4
Skill #4—Be an Opportunity-Digger

A few weeks ago, I was sitting in the back of an Uber, listening to a podcast and minding my own business, when something slipped out of my mouth and earned me a funny look from my driver.

I was listening to a podcast interview with a well-known CMO and I got so excited because they said something that really resonated with me: "You don't deserve a raise for doing your job. You get paid to do your job. If you do it, you won't get fired."

"Yes!" I exclaimed.

That was my reaction because I know there is a misconception amongst employees that career advancement is a given, it's something you are entitled to for doing your job and for sticking around. Here's the thing though, it doesn't work that way anymore. Nowadays your career is your responsibility.

You could be doing an amazing job in your current role—meeting deadlines, hitting goals, and completing all of your duties—and yet, that won't be enough to really stand out and eventually go from where you are now to where you want to be. Doing your job well merely demonstrates that you are capable of doing it. In today's competitive market, that's simply table stakes, if you want to keep your job. There are no awards for just doing what you were hired to do.

Your career advancement is in your hands. It is up to you to initiate, uncover growth opportunities, and take action towards your next role. Sticking to what you do is fine, if you want to stay where you are, but if you want to progress and get promoted, it is up to you to demonstrate your potential to step up to the next level.

So, how exactly do you create such opportunities? Being an opportunity-digger starts with understanding that your job description is just a starting point. Most people assume that the scope of their role is defined by what's written in a document, but that's a misleading perception. Yes, you were hired to do a specific job, but if you use a broader lens, for just a second, you'll be able to see that you were hired to help the company succeed. No matter how junior or senior your role is, it still serves that same purpose. When you realize and accept that your role is bigger than your job description, you'll be able to free your mind to look for growth opportunities.

Digging for opportunities is not a passive task. You can't wait for opportunities to present themselves; you need to create them. As weird as it may sound, you can actually do that.

You can create opportunities for yourself by applying a few simple tactics.

This is one of the only times where the overused catch phrase from the movie *Field of Dreams*—"If you build it, they will come"— actually makes sense. When it comes to career opportunities, if you build it, they will come. If you take the time to think about creating opportunities, you will inevitably come up with a few ideas. What's more, through this process, you will be able to identify what skills you need to develop to get to the next level. The opportunities you'll create will be designed to close your skills gap and help you become the person you need to be for your next job.

The most successful employees and team members I know are proactive. This is what they do: they decide what they want to achieve and then they create the opportunities to make it happen. They take on more than what is described in their job description, so they have the ability to learn something new and deliver more value. Over time, their teammates and managers learn to come to them with bigger and better projects, thus giving them even more opportunities to grow.

There are two types of opportunities you can develop: an opportunity to gain experience and develop new skills, or an opportunity to take on important, big, highly visible projects that will allow you to present meaningful results and gain respect and recognition. Depending on where you are starting from and what you are trying to achieve, you'll need to create one or both types of opportunities for yourself. The process is quite similar, but the end goal is different.

What does a good opportunity look like?

In order to decide which opportunity to create, you must first define your goal.

Are you looking for a promotion? Do you want to lead a team? Are you interested in developing new skills or learning a new discipline? Do you want to have more visibility and recognition to build your reputation?

In order to achieve your goal, you first need to define what success looks like. That's the best way to identify the opportunities that are going to be valuable for your career.

In general, good opportunities will push you outside of your comfort zone and allow you to stretch yourself, in order to achieve your goal. An opportunity to do more of what you are already doing is not an opportunity at all. It's an additional workload that will keep you exactly where you are. Don't be tempted to take on more work just to be busy or helpful. Remember, it's better to be the person who gets the *right* things done, than the one who gets *everything* done.

If you are focused on learning a new skill or gaining experience, do something you haven't done before, such as something that you are not fully qualified to do. Most people do not realize it, but it is extremely beneficial to stretch yourself before you officially move into a new role. Think about it: even if you fail, you fail at something that isn't part of your core responsibility. It probably won't put you at risk of losing your job but it will allow you to experiment and learn. Therefore, you have nothing to lose and everything to gain!

If, on the other hand, your goal is to gain credibility, you need to focus on opportunities that play to your strengths. You want to knock it out of the park and present exceptional results. The best way to do that is to do what you do best and make it public. You will still need to go beyond your job description, but you will be doing work you know how to do. In this particular case, you can do more of what you know how to do because you will be recognized for the extraordinary results and for going the extra mile.

It is important to remember that creating opportunities is an ongoing process. If you are aware that you need to create them and you know what kind of opportunities could be beneficial, the next step is to start brainstorming for ideas. To make it easier for you to get into the habit of opportunity-digging, I outlined a few things you could do to help accelerate this process.

1: Be a proactive opportunity-digger.

It's hard to recognize new opportunities when you're constantly immersed in life's daily chores. Designate time to step away from day-to-day pressures, so that you can think about the kind of opportunities you need to advance your career. And hey, I don't mean someday—I mean *now*. Carve out time on your calendar to think about your goals and how to create opportunities for yourself. Don't just wing it and hope brilliant ideas will magically find their way to you, because they won't. Be proactive.

Being an opportunity-digger is all about identifying strategic opportunities that will allow you to grow your career while supporting the company. To identify these types of opportunities, ask yourself a few questions:

What do you know about the business, company, or industry that only you can see? What are some possibilities your company or team haven't explored yet? Why haven't they been considered? What gaps have you identified through your interactions with others? What business objectives are you most passionate about at your company? Which of those are you uniquely qualified to help with?

Alternatively, you can focus on the skills you want to gain, and try and come up with tangible ideas on how to get them. For example: *How can I gain more leadership experience right now? Who in the company may need help with their analytics? How can I get more visibility with the leadership team? Can I help them in any way?*

Asking "big picture questions" may lead to opportunities to work cross-functionally and deliver more value to the company outside of your current role. It could also lead to a new initiative you want to run by yourself. As long as you are going to benefit from acting on such an opportunity (meaning you will gain a new skill that you need and not just take someone else's grunt work), go ahead and pursue it!

2: Always be "in the know."

A great way to find opportunities is to be interested in what's happening with the company and the industry, not just your role. When you know how the business works, how clients are attained, and how revenue is generated, you can figure out how your work contributes to the bottom line. Think outside of your own role and scope of responsibility, when you are looking for opportunities. Listen to your managers and colleagues, and read cross-company updates and reports, to always be "in the know." Seriously, if you have broad knowledge about the company, the industry, and your competitors, you'll be able to come up with better ideas for opportunities. The combination of a big-picture view and your day-to-day work will allow you to connect dots other people may not see.

If you've created your growth machine, you should already have most of this information in your inbox!

3: Invest in building relationships.

I have always been jealous of people who find it easy to socialize. They walk into a room and 10 minutes later, they know everyone's name and they are the life of the party—even when it's a work party. I used to think networking was overrated and I'd be fine without it, but that is not really the case. About halfway through my career, I learned how important it is to network and build relationships, regardless of if you work for a large corporation or a small startup. Engaging with colleagues is one of the most effective ways to identify growth opportunities, accelerate your onboarding, and gain support for your initiatives.

During my first month at Microsoft, I had to go on a business trip. I had two days of meetings scheduled, so I planned on making it a short trip. When I was discussing my plans with a colleague, he suggested that I extend the trip and make it a full week. It was my first time visiting Microsoft's headquarters in Redmond and he thought I should make the most out of this opportunity. I had no idea what he meant, but I decided to follow his advice.

I didn't know anyone in Redmond, apart from the few meetings that were scheduled for me. Not only was I new to the company, I was flying to a different country where I didn't know anyone! What was I supposed to do, reach out to strangers and ask them to meet me for coffee?

Yes. That's exactly what I was supposed to do, and that is exactly what I did.

First, I asked a few of my colleagues to recommend teams or individuals I should talk to. Some of the people I worked with had been with the company for more than a decade, and they knew everyone. Next, I used Microsoft's organization chart to identify people in similar or adjacent roles to mine, and then I sent them a cold email introducing myself and asking to meet them for coffee. Eight out of 10 people accepted my invitation and were happy to tell me about their role.

I was excited to learn more about Microsoft, but I was also terrified. What was I going to talk about? Luckily, between introductions and listening to them laying out their career stories, I was able to go through an entire conversation without needing to have something super smart to say. I also took notes and followed up with everyone, to make sure they remembered my name.

My colleague knew I needed to build a network, in order to truly succeed in my role. He explained that it was crucial to have eyes and ears in the mother ship, as we often needed to get approvals from headquarters. He was right. As a result of my quarterly meetings at Redmond, more than a few opportunities developed. From cross-functional collaborations to job offers, those relationships had a big impact on my career.

4: Ask for opportunities.

Here is a sad truth: your manager doesn't think about you and your career growth all day, every day. I know, it's a shocker. It's not that they don't care—they do—but career development doesn't drive revenue, so it's not always their top priority. And to be honest, even if they had a process in place to discuss advancement, they can't always tell if you are ready for more, unless you tell them what "more" looks like for you.

This is where you can step in and create an opportunity. Tell your manager you want to do more. Walk them through your plan and explain what kind of opportunities you are looking for. Better yet, come prepared with suggestions on how to gain the skills you need so all they need to do is say yes. Good managers want their employees to grow and succeed. They know a great team reflects on their abilities as leaders, so they are happy to help their team members advance. Even if they can't offer you an opportunity right now, you want them to know that you are ready, willing, and able to do more. You never know what could happen. Your manager has access to privileged information you are not exposed to, which means they can identify opportunities you won't know about.

A few years ago, I helped launch the Customer Support team at Colu, an early-stage startup I worked for. I hired the Head of Support and guided her as her Direct Manager. A few months into the role, she confided in me what her career goals were. She wanted to manage a team and work on her leadership skills.

At the time, I couldn't offer the headcount she needed to become a manager, but I made it my mission to find other ways to give her the responsibility she wanted.

At first, I asked her to manage external suppliers. I gave her the freedom to make purchase decisions and manage every aspect of work with our vendors. When I heard from the head of HR that a few students had reached out to ask about internship opportunities, I immediately suggested that we take on an intern to give us a hand with customer support. We needed an extra pair of hands to manage the increasing demand and this was a great opportunity to give my team member the leadership experience she needed. Later on, that intern moved to a full-time role and the Head of Support officially became a Manager.

What do opportunities look like in real life?

Let's take this discussion from theory to practice, with a few examples of career goals and the opportunities you can create to achieve them.

Let's say you are eyeing a promotion. You want to prepare yourself for your manager's role, so when they are promoted and an opportunity presents itself, you will be the most qualified candidate. For the record, you can make the jump by going to another company, but you will still need to gain the experience you are missing. Start by identifying your gap. What type of skill or experience is required to get that promotion that you lack? For this example, let's assume you need to learn how to develop strategic plans.

You have a few options here:

1) Talk to your manager and ask them to delegate more strategic work to you or to include you in their process (perhaps by shadowing them), so you could learn from their experience.
2) Take an online course, read a book, and educate yourself on the topic. Once you have theoretic experience, try to find opportunities to apply that knowledge.
3) Review the strategic plans your team has in place and try to find missed opportunities that can add value. Create a short pitch you can present to your manager, and offer to do the work yourself. Make sure your plan doesn't come through as criticism towards your manager. You want to avoid coming off as condescending. Focus on adding value, to get a foot in the door. Later on, ask to be officially included in the planning process.
4) Partner with another team in the organization and offer to "exchange" skills. You'll enhance your existing skills and have a chance to learn new ones. For example, as a marketer, you can offer the Product Team help with writing product descriptions in exchange for participating in their product development process.

Another goal could be to gain leadership experience. It could be quite challenging to gain this type of experience without being promoted to manager level, but there are a few alternatives that could give you the experience you need.

1) Leadership is not just about having the authority to tell other people what to do. In fact, leadership has nothing to do with bossing people around. Leadership is about being able to motivate and inspire others. Find a way to become the person on your team that can pull people across different departments and get everyone to work together.
2) If you are eyeing a leadership position, you probably already have some professional experience. That means you have skills you can teach others. If you want to gain some hands-on leadership experience, offer to mentor junior employees that could benefit from your knowledge and experiences. Make a real investment in their success and help them make noticeable progress. Their success will make your efforts noticeable.
3) Develop a cross-functional project that you could lead. This is a tricky one, because you have to find a real business problem that could be solved by a cross-functional team. Coming up with a good idea for a project may be time-consuming because you'll need to learn about different teams, but you should do that anyway, to learn how the business works. You can also recruit other team members to help you come up with ideas. As long as you end up running the operation and being the face of that initiative, it doesn't matter who came up with the idea.

Opportunities without execution are just dreams.

Your current role is an opportunity to stretch yourself and get out of your comfort zone while having a safety net. You can and should take steps to actively identify opportunities to learn new skills. This will boost your growth and self-confidence, leading to others having confidence in you as well. But identifying these opportunities is not enough. You need to act on them and deliver exceptional results.

Even though the opportunity you identified may be out of your scope, you still need to do the work well to get noticed and earn the credit you need to get to the next level. Opportunity-digging is a process that takes time, but the results are undeniably valuable. It's the best way to get on-the-job training for the skills that you care about the most.

The majority of employees don't think about creating opportunities; they just wait for them to happen. Invaluable employees create their own opportunities at work and then go and crush it with execution.

Chapter 4 Checklist and Summary

How to be an opportunity-digger and create opportunities at work:

1. Proactively seek opportunities—set time on your calendar
2. Define your goal and what you are trying to achieve
3. Always be "in the know"
4. Invest in building relationships
5. Ask for opportunities—For example, use your current job to gain the experience you need for your next role.
    ❏ Volunteer internally
    ❏ Initiate a project

- ❏ Offer to take the load off of your manager
- ❏ Seek mentorship
- ❏ Help others
- ❏ Do an internal internship, to trade your existing skills for opportunities to learn new ones

INVALUABLE

Chapter 5
Skill #5—Become a Fixer

When I was consulting for Google, I spent a lot of time in the office with the team I was supporting. At the time, most team members were working from the same office I was assigned to, while the managers were working remotely. Spending time with the team daily for a few months allowed me to identify a problem that was beyond my scope of work. I was hired to consult about marketing, but the problem I had identified was about culture and leadership—and it was a problem that affected the entire team, not just the marketing department.

From where I was standing, it became clear the team had some communication issues. Information wasn't flowing from the top in a consistent and transparent way. As a result, the extended team felt disconnected and frustrated. Many teams at Google work remotely because they include employees from different states and even different countries. It's a great way to build a diverse and inclusive team, but that type of structure can also be challenging, like in this case.

I could have easily stayed out of it. I wasn't an employee, so what gave me the right to bring up an internal problem?

If that is what you are thinking, you are absolutely right. No one asked me to do it, nor was it part of my job description, but I identified a problem and felt the need to fix it.

It wasn't about me. It was about the team. I joined to help the team become more successful, regardless of how I was going to make that happen, so I decided to take action.

I put together a plan that outlined the problem and offered solutions that would help improve the team's communications while working remotely. No one likes to hear they have a problem, so it is better to have an honest conversation face-to-face, rather than send an email. I scheduled a meeting with the group manager and walked him through my observations, to drive the message home.

The group manager listened carefully, asked me questions, and eventually thanked me for bringing the problem to his attention. He then gave me the green light to immediately start executing alongside his management team.

The remote communications plan was a success, and within a few weeks, the team saw meaningful improvements in their ability to communicate and work collaboratively.

When you make it your mission to solve problems for other people, even when it's not your job, it means you are assuming the role of the fixer. Most leaders I know appreciate problem-solvers and despise blame-shifters (you know, the kind of people who never do anything wrong and constantly blame everyone and everything for their mistakes).

A fixer knows that success is not just about them and their job. Success depends on every person in the company doing their job efficiently and effectively. Fixers volunteer to solve problems for their colleagues and managers, when they have the opportunity to do so.

The role of the fixer takes different shapes, as you progress in your career. When you are a junior employee, solving problems is the most efficient way to get noticed, gain experience, and deliver value. I used to joke about it and say you should be walking around, asking people how you can help them all day long. However, that description is not far from the truth. You should find ways to use your experience and know how to be helpful.

At whatever stage you are at in your career, you should focus on being the most helpful person in the room. It will help you build trust and gain credibility. Also, make sure you have the capacity to follow through when you offer to help, because solving problems takes time and you still have a job to do. You don't want to be in a situation where you over-promise and under-deliver. That's a really good way to create a bad impression.

As you become more senior, solving problems becomes more and more strategic. It's less about getting something done and more about getting to the root cause of complex problems, especially when you want to optimize processes, generate revenue, or reduce costs. Those problems usually affect a larger number of people, ranging from a department to the entire company, and solving them usually requires a little more experience.

However, solving problems isn't everything. Finding them is important, too!

I recently interviewed a sales executive about his career. I asked him to share the advice he would give his younger self.

He said, "I used to think that solving problems is a super power and if I know how to do that, I'll be in good shape. As I got more experience, I realized it's not just solving problems that is important; it's the ability to identify those problems to begin with. If you can see that a problem exists and are willing to run towards the fire to help solve it, that is what makes you indispensable to the company."

He totally nailed it with that observation. When you solve problems someone else told you to solve, you are providing a tactical solution and you get shit done—and anyone can do that. However, when you are able to identify a problem by yourself, it makes your work strategic. You do something that most people can't or won't do, and that makes you stand out.

So, how can you identify problems?

If you are not actually going to run around and ask everyone how you can help, how are you going to be able to find problems? Well, you'll need to go hunting for problems, and there are a few easy ways you can do that.

1: Identify pains

Pains (sometimes called "pain points") are usually opportunities to drive change and improve. Essentially, they are indicative of a problem waiting to be solved. If you pay attention, you'll be able to identify pains quite easily.

Complaints, rants, and frustration are all signs of pain. They are easily detected because people like to express their pain. If something is inherently wrong, it will likely keep coming up again and again. Spend time engaging in casual hallway conversations, reading customer support tickets, and simply asking some of your colleagues how they are doing.

I was able to identify a pattern at Google when a few employees shared the same frustrations again and again, on various occasions. Different individuals mentioned how the lack of communication was affecting their ability to deliver the best results in their respective roles. After hearing it a few times, it was clear it was a real problem, not just an individual rant.

If you want to be more proactive about problem-hunting, you can also ask your manager what keeps them up at night. You may be able to help just by listening. Better yet, you'll be able to use your skills to solve their problem.

I once asked my manager how I could help make their life easier. The answer wasn't at all what I expected. My manager was an executive who traveled quite often. They probably spent more time traveling than at home, and it was taking its toll. They wanted to spend less time traveling and more time with their family. At the time, I was responsible for coordinating all of their speaking engagements and public appearances. Therefore, I knew I could influence some of their plans through my work. Once I became aware of the problem, I was able to make changes to cut down on travel and batch their speaking opportunities, so they could make the most out of every trip. I also became a better gatekeeper. I stopped saying yes to every speaking opportunity and focused on the ones that had the biggest impact. In the end, my manager was happier, their family was happier, and I earned their trust and appreciation. I didn't solve a business problem per se, but I fixed a shitty situation, which earned me credit—a lot of credit.

2: Find ways to increase efficiency

Do you remember the scene from the animated Disney movie *Zootopia*, where Nick and Judy go to the DMV? Watching them wait for their clerk, who was a sloth, to finish a sentence was cringeworthy. (Ironically, his name was Flash!) While the scene was funny, it was also a metaphor for the inefficiency that is associated with the far from perfect service one would expect from the DMV.

How many times have you heard one of your colleagues complain about a long or annoying process? How many times have you protested, when you've had to use old software? Whether it's manually updating spreadsheets or having to go through five people to get a sign-off for a project, I can assure you there is a better and more efficient way to get things done.

Efficiency saves time and money, and more importantly, it removes a lot of frustrations. Fixing inefficient issues is a great way to earn friends for life.

You can identify inefficiencies by experiencing them or by talking to people. You can also initiate a quest to find inefficiencies by evaluating the effectiveness of different company processes and tools. That approach may take longer, but it could have the potential to make a bigger impact.

Whatever you do, start by verifying that this is more than one person's problem. If you work for a small company and you can make your CEO or CFO happier by suggesting a better process, by all means, go for it. You will be a hero. But if your company has thousands of employees, you should aim for a solution that could impact more than one person.

Once you have identified an inefficiency, the next step is to fix it. Hopefully, you picked up on that inefficiency because you realized there is a better way to get things done. Perhaps you have seen a particular process elsewhere and experienced it being much more efficient. In that case, your next step is to present the solution to the relevant stakeholder, or take action to fix it yourself.

If it is a problem you have never encountered before, you can do some research to find the best solution. You will help the company become more productive and learn a new skill in the process. However, if you decide to fix an inefficiency you have never encountered before, try to make sure the skills that are required to fix it are relevant to your career. There is no reason for you to invest in learning how to code if you have no intention of using that skill in the near future!

3: Do proactive opportunity-digging

The same processes that can help you identify opportunities can also be used to identify inefficiencies. Keep yourself in the know, talk to people, and build relationships. All of these tactics apply for opportunity-digging as well as finding and fixing problems because more often than not, problems are opportunities in disguise.

Now that you've identified some problems, how can you fix them?

You did the hard work, you listened, you poked, and you found a problem. You are already ahead of most people, but spotting a problem is not enough. Now it's time to turn this problem into an opportunity by actually fixing it.

1: View problems through a new lens.

"Houston, we have a problem." When you hear that sentence, you know you are in trouble. You know something bad is going to happen.

A problem is perceived as a bad thing, and an opportunity is viewed as a good thing. It's how our brain categorizes past experiences.

"Houston, we have an opportunity" makes you feel quite differently.

Changing the terminology by using the word "opportunity" instead of "problem" will help change your approach and your perspective. Instead of telling yourself you have an obstacle ahead of you, you can motivate yourself by thinking what overcoming that obstacle could look like.

Each time you encounter a problem, practice seeing it as a chance to improve.

As simple as it may sound, ask yourself: *How could this problem become an opportunity? How could this situation be the best thing that ever happened to me or to the company?*

During my time at SodaStream, we decided to make a massive investment in marketing and run a Super Bowl ad. We wanted to reach a broad audience and gain exposure for our flagship product—the at-home soda machine. We spent countless hours coming up with a unique, creative script for the ad—one that we knew would get the attention we were hoping to gain. We recruited an A-list star, Scarlett Johansson, to be the spokesperson for the ad, and we paid the outrageous amount that is required to buy the air time. After months of work, we got some bad news. Our ad didn't comply with Super Bowl guidelines, so it was disqualified. After everything we had put into the production, we were not going to be able to get the air time, unless we changed the ad!

The team was gutted, morale was low, and we were all exhausted—after weeks of working around the clock to bring to life the most ambitious campaign we had ever worked on.

Then, something amazing happened. We asked ourselves: *How can this be the best thing that ever happened to us?* We tried to find the opportunity instead of focusing on the problem, and we came up with a genius solution. We decided to tell people that our ad was disqualified. We'd make it public and gain the attention we wanted by showing up as the underdog.

Within a few days, we put together a new marketing plan that focused on driving pre-game buzz. Instead of competing for air time during the game, we grabbed attention in the days leading up to the game. The result was better than we could have expected and included dozens of articles in mainstream media, more than 15 million views online for the disqualified ad, and tons of buzz on social media. We had successfully turned a massive problem into an opportunity.

Sometimes, seeing a problem through a new lens (of opportunity) is all that is required to fix it.

2: Figure it out.

I've already written about adopting a learner's mindset and building a growth machine to help you become a lifelong learner. Here, you are going to put those skills to use. You are going to figure out how to solve a problem you have never faced before, simply by figuring it out.

You can do some research, read a guide or a book, talk to experts and colleagues, or listen to a podcast. Whatever you are facing, I'm 99.9% sure someone has already figured it out and all you need to do is follow their lead.

You can't solve every problem, so focus on the ones that are just a few degrees of separation from your core skills, not the ones that require you to learn a completely new profession.

3: Collaborate.

Teamwork makes the dream work. I learned this important lesson from the CEO at Colu. I was juggling too many balls and trying to solve too many problems at the time. I was the only marketer at the company and I was determined to drive the expected business results as a one-woman show. Apparently, my drive was making me blind and stupid. I was operating in a silo, making decisions without consulting the other teams, and it wasn't working well. I had too many problems and not nearly enough time.

During one of our weekly meetings, the CEO leaned back and said, "You know, you are not supposed to solve all of these problems on your own. You can't keep working yourself into the ground. You are a part of a team and it's time you let them in."

For a minute, I was taken aback. I thought I was doing a good job holding down the fort. *Why was he criticizing my work? If I'm the head of marketing, shouldn't I be making all of the decisions? After all, I was the only one with marketing experience, so shouldn't it be my call?* I was a little upset and it was clouding my judgment. I was being defensive instead of actually listening.

Later that day, after I had the opportunity to process everything, I realized the CEO was right. I didn't have any fellow marketers to consult, but I still had a team to collaborate and solve problems with. It was hard to accept, but I didn't have to figure everything out on my own. I could work with the extended team to solve marketing problems and it wouldn't take anything away from my responsibilities as a leader. Eventually, the insight I got from the sales team and the data I received from the product team allowed me to make better decisions, work efficiently, and deliver better results.

Here is the bottom line: if you are trying to solve a problem and you are stuck or need feedback, reach out to your team. They will most likely take it as a compliment that you chose to seek their advice, and they will be happy to collaborate and offer their feedback.

Also, don't forget to give collaborators credit when it's due. You may be the one solving the problem, but it's important to recognize it was a team effort. It won't take anything away from your achievement. Instead, it will position you as a leader who knows how to mobilize others.

4: Use lateral thinking to find a creative solution.

Early in my career, when I worked for a PR agency, our specialty was helping startups get their product or service featured in top tech blogs. We were the best. Seriously. We had a detailed, tried-and-true process that helped us secure coverage every single time. Well, almost every single time.

One of my clients developed a tool that helped people create online greeting cards. It was a cool product that allowed customers to easily create a beautifully designed digital greeting card and send it to friends and family. It was sleek, convenient, and fun to use.

As far as I was concerned, pitching it was going to be easy. What's not to like?

I was wrong. For the first time in a long time, we couldn't sell the story. Every writer we approached declined to write about the company. We tried a few different angles and we approached different reporters, but nothing worked.

It was almost time to let the client know we were not able to do the job we were hired to do, which was not a conversation I was looking forward to having. Eventually, the fear of admitting failure got my creative juices flowing and I came up with one last Hail Mary.

My idea was quite simple. I decided to focus on one person: the managing editor at Mashable, the top tech blog at the time. I knew if Mashable published a story, the rest would follow, so I decided to "go big or go home."

I knew that sending a simple email wouldn't do the job. We had already tried that and failed. So, I had to find a different approach that would be so creative and outrageous that it could work.

It was a week before Valentine's Day—the perfect time to send a very special Valentine to the Mashable's editor. We decided to have some fun and tease the editor about his good looks. The guy was a bit of a celebrity with a large following on social media and a not-so-small ego.

We used the client's product to create an amusing greeting card featuring the editor, then we sent it to the entire editorial team at Mashable. I was hoping one of the reporters would jump on the opportunity to make fun of their boss.

It worked!

One of the senior reporters decided to share the card on their Facebook profile and it blew up. Then, the editor joined the conversation and shared the card on his profile as well. To my surprise, he mentioned my client's company, to give them credit for the funny prank.

Those social media mentions drove hundreds of visits to the website and eventually allowed us to get the PR coverage we needed. We ended up solving the problem in a nonconventional way, because the logical way of thinking didn't work. We tried everything we considered to be a best practice, but we couldn't get the result we wanted. That was where lateral thinking came into play.

Lateral thinking is the ability to approach problems in a creative, non-conventional way.

We are all trained to think logically, to collect information, identify accepted conventions, and draw a straight line that leads to an answer. It's how our brain is wired to work so it can reduce processing time and operate more efficiently. Logical thinking prevents us from having to re-evaluate every decision we make and allows us to learn from experience and develop best practices. However, when you are faced with a unique problem, when circumstances change, or when you have constraints, logic doesn't always provide a viable solution. That is when you need to break away from traditional modes of thinking, discarding established patterns and preconceived notions, in order to make a breakthrough.

Imagine you are doing some renovations in your bathroom when suddenly your hammer slips and falls on your toilet, breaking a big chunk off. What do you do? Some people may call a repairman, and others may try and fix the toilet themselves or order a new one, but I'm willing to bet that most of you won't solve this problem by opening a pack of Ramen noodles! You read that right. A pack of ramen noodles to fix a broken toilet? Most people wouldn't think to do that, but a DIY enthusiast from China decided to try it out and it worked. Now, I'm not saying that it's a great idea. I don't know how resilient a toilet is if it's made out of noodles, but it is definitely a creative solution.

When you apply lateral thinking to a problem at work, you want to make sure it's not only creative but also effective. The unconventional idea you come up with has to be functional, to deliver valuable results.

If you want to train your brain to solve problems using reasoning that is not immediately obvious, you will need to be deliberate about it. You'll need to practice being able to come up with ideas that may not surface using traditional, step-by-step logic.

Here are five particular methods that could help you start flexing your lateral thinking muscles:

1: Look for alternatives.—When conventional logical solutions come to mind, list them, and then look for alternatives. Deliberately ignoring perfectly good but straightforward solutions will enable you to find paths you would otherwise miss. Make a commitment to find at least three different ways to solve the problem you are facing that are not obvious. Even if initially it seems there are no alternative solutions, stick with it, because you will find those alternatives, eventually. You can use a mind map to brainstorm ideas or ask colleagues and friends for their opinion, to gain a different perspective.

2: Think about the problem from a first-principle perspective.—If you find it difficult to ignore the conventional straightforward solution, try stripping the problem down to its most basic elements. As you may recall, the idea behind first-principle thinking is to remove any and all constraints and assumptions you may have unconsciously applied in your thinking process.

In the story I shared, the original problem was getting PR coverage, but that wasn't the underlying problem. The company needed to gain awareness to attract new customers. Getting featured on a top tier publication was one way to do that, but not the only way.

Knowing that gave me something to work with. Getting PR coverage was only a means to an end. When I identified the real problem, I was able to find another way to get scaled exposure within the services my company was able to provide.

3: Find the worst possible solution.—This is a creative exercise that we often use in marketing, to come up with innovative campaign ideas. It's basically a brainstorming session that requires you to find the worst possible solutions to your problem. You need to go crazy here and take it to extremes.

We once used this technique to come up with a creative campaign to promote a superhero movie. One of the suggestions was a competition in which people would try jumping off of a building, to prove they can fly. If you were alive at the end of the competition, you won. That is an example of the level of "bad" I'm talking about.

Thinking about bad solutions forces you to ignore biases and constraints. When you know the ideas you come up with won't be relevant anyway, you stop criticizing yourself, and that's when creativity kicks in. This exercise takes away the risk of getting it wrong. It eliminates inhibitions. That's why it works.

4: Change your state.—Often, when we focus on solving a problem, we get trapped in our own rabbit hole. When it seems like you can't think of anything else because your brain keeps coming up with the same answers, take a break. Change your environment, go outside, listen to music, or read a book. Find a random stimulation that will keep your conscious mind from thinking about the problem and distract you from logical thinking. After you have had some time to disconnect, you should be able to look at your problem with a fresh perspective.

5: Gain a wide variety of experiences.—Have you ever heard of the 10,000-hour rule? It's a principle that says in order to become a world class expert at something, you need to spend at least 10,000 hours practicing it. While I don't disagree that practice makes perfect, I think there are additional factors to take into account, particularly when it comes to career success. Deliberate repetition will definitely sharpen your skills, but it might affect your ability to think laterally and be creative.

The best way I know to think outside of the box is to play outside of the box. The more diverse your life experiences, the more you'll be able to see patterns and parallels across seemingly unrelated fields.

Your brain works like a sponge. Even if it doesn't feel like you are able to process everything you are exposed to, your brain soaks up everything and processes it, behind the scenes (subconsciously). The more you feed your brain with different experiences, the more resources it will have to go through when it searches through the information in your head.

Don't be afraid to enrich your life with a variety of experiences. Explore what interests you and piques your curiosity at work and in your personal life, and expand your internal search results. Doing that will come in handy when your brain tries to come up with creative solutions.

Developing a fixer mindset will help you become invaluable.

Great fixers consciously look for problems because they want to remove obstacles that may prevent the company from succeeding. Fixers identify problems. They also take the time to fix them, instead of looking the other way, like most people. Fixers believe that they can and should take initiative to proactively solve problems, even if they fall out of their scope of work.

Being a fixer is about removing roadblocks and increasing productivity for your team and company, in order to help everyone around you deliver better results. The desire to fix problems hinges on your ability to think like an owner and take immediate actions to optimize for the long term.

Chapter 5 Checklist and Summary

How to identify problems:
- ❏ Find pains
- ❏ Find ways to increase efficiency
- ❏ Do proactive opportunity-digging

How to solve problems:
- ❏ View problems as opportunities
- ❏ Figure it out
- ❏ Collaborate
- ❏ Use lateral thinking to find a creative solution

1. Look for alternatives
2. Think about the problem from a first-principle perspective
3. Find the worst possible solution
4. Change your state
5. Gain a wide variety of experiences

Chapter 6
Skill #6—Become a Master Influencer

I once stopped a plane from taking off.

I stood on the tarmac, waving my hands frantically, in an attempt to get the pilot's attention. I could see one of the security guards running towards me, to get me out of there, but I didn't stop. Instead, I started jumping up and down, waving my hands faster, hoping the pilot would notice. My heart was pounding and I was out of breath, but I knew I had to do it. I had to stop the plane long enough to get two more passengers on board the aircraft.

As much as I wish that was how it happened, I actually *did* stop a plane from taking off, but it wasn't as dramatic in real life.

I was a few thousands of miles away from the airport at the time, and the only tool I had was a phone. I was manning the 24/7 customer support desk at the travel agency, when a call came in from a passenger. He was about to board a flight in Italy but realized he was in the wrong terminal. With less than 30 minutes to takeoff, he wasn't sure he and his wife would make it, but they had to try, because they had to attend a funeral. The couple had been on vacation when they heard a family member passed away, and they were now making their way back home. They were so desperate to make it on time, they were already running when they called me for help.

It was crunch time. I had to reach the gate and convince the purser to delay closing the doors, even though it was against regulations and could potentially get them in trouble. I didn't have time to think; I had to act.

I picked up the phone and made the call. Four, five, six rings. Finally, someone picked up.

"Gate 107, this is Kate," the voice said.

"Hi, Kate, this is Maya. Quick question: did you lose two passengers?"

"Yes," Kate answered. "Do you know where they are?"

"I do. They are on their way to you, as we speak," I relayed, in my most confident voice.

"I can't wait any longer. I have to close the doors now," she said.

"I'll be honest with you, Kate. We need your help. They are going home to say goodbye to a loved one that had just passed away."

Kate hesitated for a second but then repeated what she had previously told me. "I'm sorry, it's too late. I have to close the doors now."

Kate was about to hang up on me, so I made my last move. "You know, it's the last flight of the day. If they miss it, you'll have to get them on the first flight out tomorrow. I can see that it's sold out, so it will be a mess."

It was quiet for a second and then I heard her talking to the crew on the airplane, saying "I found the missing passengers, but I need a few more minutes. Would we still make it out on time?"

I guess the answer on the other side was yes because Kate got back to me and said, "They had better be here in the next five minutes or I'm closing the gate."

"They'll be there," I promised.

I don't know if it was my convincing argument or the fact I kept her on the phone and away from the doors long enough, but my passengers made it. They boarded that plane and got to say goodbye to their loved one.

I can't know for sure what convinced Kate to help me, but I have a theory. I put myself in Kate's shoes and tried to think about what could be important enough to convince her to break the rules. I knew it wasn't going to be Kate's kind heart. You see, the life of a flight attendant isn't as glamorous as most people think. They are constantly bombarded with complaints and requests, and it's their job to smile and provide service, while following a list of strict aviation rules. That means flight attendants need to learn how to say no more often than they say yes, in order to put safety first. It sounds a bit heartless, but when you deal with people's lives, it is necessary.

I also knew the airline would lose money if the passengers didn't get on their booked flight since the airline would be obligated to offer them seats on the next available flight—seats someone else could be paying for.

I tried to appeal to Kate's emotions when I told her about the funeral. I gave her a chance to be the hero under the circumstances, but with the pressure she had on the ground right before the plane took off, she wasn't motivated to help. However, when I flipped the script and explained how keeping the doors open could benefit her and the airline, I got her attention.

The story you tell people is the key to successfully influencing them. Understanding people and where they are coming from is the secret sauce for getting a buy-in, collaborating, and leading without authority. Building relationships and getting to know the people you approach is how you craft a story (also called "influence narrative") that motivates them to help you.

When you seek to influence people, you can craft a story that appeals to people's logical, emotional, and cooperative needs. If you are going for a logical and rational story, you'll have to present an argument that outlines the benefits on the organizational level, the personal level, or both. If you choose to focus on an emotional story, you'll need to touch people in a deeply personal manner, so you'll need to understand their values, feelings, and desires. If your story is all about cooperation, you'll need to outline a mutually important goal and demonstrate how working together could be beneficial for everyone. The key here is to remember that different people will be motivated by different incentives, so you will have to tailor your story to their needs.

Your goal in creating a great influence narrative is to present reality in a compelling way, one that serves both you and your counterpart. If you can make someone feel really good about themselves or if you can present a positive outcome that reflects on them, you'll be able to motivate people to help you.

There is a formula to creating a great influence narrative.

For the majority of my career, I didn't think I had an influence narrative, even though I was using it almost every day. I thought I was just having thoughtful conversations that resulted in me getting the approval or buy-in I needed from my colleagues, for the most part.

It was during my consulting project for Google that someone pointed out what I was doing, so I took a step back, to try and describe the method.

This is what I came up with:

Start by understanding the problem. Then, try to see the problem from the perspective of your colleagues. You can do that by asking yourself what they could get out of supporting you or what they stood to lose if they ignored your advice. When the situation calls for evidence, collect data to back up your claims, and use it to tailor the story to the needs of your colleagues.

Writing everything down made me realize I had a formula to influence others, and I have been using it for years to inspire, motivate, and eventually mobilize people to take action.

The influence formula is designed to inspire action. It incorporates facts with empathy, in order to present the story in a mutually beneficial way—one that takes into account what your colleague stands to gain when they support you.

Anyone can use this formula to influence others, but please remember this is not a sales technique or a psychological trick that is meant to guilt people into giving you what you want.

An effective influence narrative will convince your counterpart to trust you and choose to follow your lead because they identify with your story and they want to experience the positive outcome your story entails.

Here are the five elements of the influence formula:

1: Define the purpose of your story.— What goal are you trying to achieve? What is the end result your story should deliver?

2: Identify the challenge or barrier you'll need to overcome.—Why is your counterpart resistant? What are they afraid of? Why aren't they on board? What are the objections you need to overcome?

3: Identify the benefit or motivation for your counterpart.—What is in it for them? If you are successful in your actions, how will it benefit them? There must always be an upside for them, otherwise you won't get people motivated enough to take action. Focus on seeing the world from your counterpart's perspective and ask yourself how they can benefit from the situation.

4: Flip the script.—Create a new context and connect the dots, to craft a story that drives action. The idea here is to present the situation in a way that shows your counterpart how taking action towards your goal is going to benefit them or help them avoid pain.

Support your story by gathering data, collecting feedback, or doing the research needed to validate your claims. Your influence narrative will be much stronger if it is built on facts, not just your opinions.

5: Call for action.—What do they need to do to turn this narrative into a reality? It is important to make this call for action very specific. Don't just ask for help. Instead, ask them to take a specific action.

Now, let's look at a couple of examples that will make it clear how to use the formula in different situations at work.

Example 1: Motivating employees or colleagues

While consulting for Google, one of the biggest challenges I had was to get the team to shift their focus from generating outputs to driving outcomes. The challenge wasn't that they couldn't see the benefits, because they could. It was about convincing them to step out of their comfort zones and try new things. I had to convince team members to start doing things they had never done before, to go beyond their job descriptions, without offering any guarantees or incentives.

It was time to divide and conquer. I decided to focus on one team member at a time and use the influence formula to motivate them individually.

My first breakthrough happened over a casual lunch. I was sitting across from one of the team members when I asked her a seemingly simple question. I wanted to know where she wanted to be in five years' time. I was curious to hear about the career she envisioned for herself.

My lunch date saw herself taking on a creative marketing role where she could create art and drive business results through inspirational stories. It was clear she was excited about her future because her voice changed and her eyes sparkled when she spoke about it.

I then asked a follow-up question. I asked whether she knew what it took to become a creative director. This was a trick question that got my lunch date to stop and think.

"I think I'll need a portfolio," she said. "I'll need to produce a variety of content pieces that showcase my unique style and the ability of the contents to drive business results."

That was my cue to storm in with my narrative. I repeated what she said about the requirements to become a creative director, and wondered out loud whether her current role could help her build that portfolio. To make sure my words hit home, I asked her to imagine how impressive her portfolio was going to be when she demonstrated how her work reached millions of people and made an impact on the business. I asked her to imagine what a competitive advantage she would have over professionals who only focus on their art.

The message was received, loud and clear. Right after lunch, I got a calendar invite to discuss our content distribution strategy, which was the task I wanted the team to work on.

Using the five elements of the influence formula, let's break down what happened during that lunch.

1) The purpose of the story: get a team member to spend 50% of their time working on content distribution

2) What challenge needs to be overcome: she was not comfortable stepping out of her comfort zone. She was not motivated to invest time in additional work when she was not getting any complaints about her performance.

3) What's in for them: the success of the distribution campaign could influence their personal success. My goal was to figure out how. Initially, I thought it would be a great line in her resume, but after the conversation we had, it became clear that working on content

distribution would help her build a more impressive portfolio, which would allow her to pursue the career of her dreams.

4) Finding a way to flip the script: it was no longer about putting in extra effort and learning something new to benefit the company, but is now about investing time and effort, in order to gain a competitive advantage in her future career.

5) Call for action: spend time working on content distribution, to learn how to drive business results through creativity.

Example 2: Championing a new idea or getting a buy-in for your plan

Getting a buy-in is a key component in gaining opportunities to prove your value and shine. The influence formula can help you understand how to position your idea and get the support you need, even if you are trying to influence the whole company.

The first thing I wanted to know when I joined Colu to lead marketing was who the target audience was. I had to identify the customers we were targeting, in order to create a relevant marketing strategy. At that time, the company wasn't collecting data about its customers. Instead, the team was working based on the assumption that the audience was most likely young, predominantly male, tech-savvy professionals. That was the common belief, even though we didn't have any data to back up that claim. The more I snooped around, the clearer it became that no one validated those assumptions. But no matter how hard I lobbied for a data collection process during customer onboarding, I couldn't get the product team to prioritize this work.

My experience taught me that having data was the key to making any business decision, so I had to make the team see for themselves how valuable it was. It took two weeks to get everything that I needed and put a compelling story together. Eventually, I was able to influence the team. I decided to demonstrate the importance of the data we needed, by actually going out and getting that data. I sent out a survey to our existing customers and asked them to voluntarily share some personal information. I wanted to know where they were from, how old they were, what their gender was, and most importantly, why they were using our product.

I got more than enough responses to prove my point, so I put together a few slides to highlight the results, then presented my findings to the entire company. My presentation had nothing to do with the onboarding process I so desperately wanted to change. It didn't mention the tools I wanted to implement to collect data or the product team's polite refusal to prioritize the work.

My presentation was about marketing and everything I had learned about our target audience through my survey. I opened with the biggest shocker I could think of. I showed the team who our customers really were. They were in their 30s and 40s, they had families, and they held a variety of jobs, across different professions. They were not tech-savvy young professionals, as we had originally thought. This information came as a surprise for most people, evident by the gasping sounds that came from my team members.

The next slide laid out the reason our customers were using the product. Once again, the most common answer had nothing to do with our original guess.

Now, it was time to connect the dots. I shared with the team what the marketing strategy should have looked like, if it was created based on the original assumption, and then I showed them what my strategy looks like, now that I knew who our customers were and what they care about. Those plans were quite different, to say the least.

My presentation made it clear to the entire team that data had to play a major role in every company business decision, from then on.

The new onboarding process was implemented a few weeks later. As well, the entire company adopted a data-driven approach, to the point where we called out anyone who tried to justify a decision with merely a gut feeling.

How did the influence formula come into play here?

1) The purpose of the story: to get my teammates to understand the importance of data and implement a data-collection process.
2) What the problem was: it wasn't clear why the data collection process should be prioritized.
3) What's in for them: verifying that they are working on the right product for the right audience, to find a product market fit and help the company grow.
4) Finding a way to flip the script: instead of focusing on shifting blame, I focused on the value of collecting data. Instead of telling the team data collection is important, I showed them how it can affect their business decisions.
5) Call for action: develop a data-collection process to make sure we had a way to validate assumptions.

Becoming a master influencer requires interest, time, patience, and practice.

The influence formula is a powerful tool, but it could become even more valuable, if you follow a few best practices.

For starters, in order to understand people, you need to be genuinely interested in them. I can't stress that enough. People crave authenticity in their relationships, and they can spot a fake gesture from a mile away. Don't fake it. Build the relationship before you actually need something from them, and make an effort to get into their world. It can be as simple as asking how they spent their weekend or inviting them to lunch.

As I've mentioned, a well-crafted story makes people feel good about themselves. It helps them feel validated, supported, and seen. If you want to get your message across quite easily, listen to what people say and observe what they do. You'll learn what they care about and what makes them tick. Understanding your counterpart is imperative to crafting a compelling story, because it needs to deeply resonate with them.

Every influence narrative you create must be tailored to the person you are pitching, in order to be successful.

Two last things you can do to help your story land well is build rapport and position yourself as an expert. Most people (myself included) are predisposed to listen to someone they perceive as an authority. If you want to improve your chances to influence others, make sure they see you as knowledgeable on the topic you are pitching. Research and read everything you can about the subject, and use your growth machine or your professional background to make it clear you know what you are talking about.

Crafting compelling stories requires practice. While I can share the components of the formula, there is no template for flipping the script. That is something you will have to come up with on your own, because the narrative will vary, depending on your perspective, the unique situation you are in, and who you are talking to.

When you are just getting started with the formula, take the time to actually write down the steps and how you think they will play out, like I have done in the two examples provided. If possible, come up with a few creative ideas for flipping the script, then pick the one you feel is the most convincing.

The narrative formula is a strategic tool that will give you the ability to influence others throughout the organization. The best part of this strategy is that it's designed to create a win-win situation. You don't need to manipulate, backstab, or outsmart anyone. Instead of spending valuable time blaming others and complaining, you will devise a narrative that creates an opportunity for mutual success. How awesome is that?

Chapter 6 Checklist and Summary

The influence formula:
1. Define the purpose of your narrative. What goal are you trying to achieve? What is the end result your story should deliver?
2. Identify the challenge or barrier you'll need to overcome. Why is your counterpart resistant? What are they afraid of? Why aren't they on board? What are the objections you need to overcome?

3. Identify the benefit or motivation for your counterpart. What is in it for them? If you are successful in your actions, how will it benefit them? There must always be an upside for them, otherwise you won't get people motivated enough to take action. Focus on seeing the world from your counterpart's perspective and ask yourself how they can benefit from the situation.
4. Flip the script. Create a new context and connect the dots, to craft a story that drives action. The idea here is to present the situation in a way that shows your counterpart how taking action towards your goal is going to benefit them or help them avoid pain.

   Support your story by gathering data, collecting feedback, or doing the research needed to validate your claims. The influence narrative will be much stronger if it is built on facts, not just your opinions.
5. Call for action. What do they need to do to turn this narrative into a reality? It is important to make this call for action very specific. Don't just ask for help. Instead, ask them to take a specific action.

Every influence narrative you create must be tailored to the person you are pitching, in order to be successful. Relationship best practices:
- Be genuinely interested
- Understand where they are coming from
- Gain credibility as an expert

INVALUABLE

Chapter 7
Skill #7—Master the Art of Managing—Up and Across

Most of us do not work in a vacuum. We have colleagues, team members, and managers who we interact with and rely on to get our work done. We need to collaborate, share resources, and sometimes get a buy-in, in order to do our job well. That means we need to actively manage those relationships, to build trust and encourage collaboration. Somehow, that's easier said than done.

When there are no clear guidelines, roles, or responsibilities, how do you mobilize others? While friendship is an important component in building relationships and trust, it's not enough to influence and motivate people to take action. In order to manage up and across, you'll need to think more strategically about those relationships, put in the time and effort to get acquainted with your colleagues, and apply everything you learned about the influence formula in the previous chapter.

Leading without authority is a crucial skill to master if you want to accelerate your career growth, create more opportunities, and position yourself as an invaluable employee. It's not enough to be an impressive individual contributor. If you want to reach the top of the career ladder, you need to forge strong ties with your peers and managers so you can build momentum and make a meaningful impact.

It's never too early to start managing up and across because it's not a switch you can turn on and off when it suits you; it's a long-term strategy.

Managing Up

My boss at Microsoft used to tell people I was his manager, not the other way around. On paper, he was the senior leader, but in real life, I took ownership and managed quite a few processes independently, so he was kind of right.

For the most part, employees expect to take direction from their managers and be told what is expected of them. While I agree managers should provide high-level directions to their employees, I believe it is much more beneficial for employees to manage their managers and shape their own role. That is exactly what I did when I joined Microsoft.

Just a few weeks into my role, I set up a meeting with my manager, to review what I had done during my first 30 days. Yes, instead of waiting for my manager to ask for an update, I took the initiative. I used that meeting to present the progress I had made, to show what I had accomplished, and to present what I was going to do next. Instead of waiting for directions, I set the tone for our relationship from the get-go by positioning myself as a proactive, action-oriented partner. That simple step allowed me to gain my manager's trust and start a truly empowering friendship.

If you think about it, you spend more time with your manager than with nearly any other person in your life. Your relationship with your manager is the most important relationship you'll have at work, so it's one that you need to nurture and work on from the start.

You can do that by developing a strategic plan to "manage up." That means you do whatever you can to make your boss's job easier by managing your manager. The goal is to make it simple for them to think through challenges and make decisions. You can do that by providing information while making a lot of small decisions on your own. Although you have a job description with personal responsibilities, your ultimate goal is to support your boss's success. When they look good, you look good to the organization, and vice versa. Managers look for people who make them look like rock stars, not people who require micromanagement and end up dragging them down.

The first step to building a great relationship with your manager is to intentionally get to know them as a person. I'm not saying you need to become BFFs, but you should get a sense for who they are as people. Where did they come from? How did they get to where they are in their career? What drives them? What are they passionate about? Make it a two-way conversation and share information about yourself, to build trust and encourage them to open up. Simple questions that help you get to know one another can go a long way toward helping you understand what makes your boss tick (and what ticks them off), so you can communicate with them effectively.

The next step is to get familiar with your manager's goals, objectives, and desired outcomes. If you aren't clear on those things, now's the time to set up a one-on-one meeting to fix that. You need to know such things because their goals are essentially your goals. Everything you do is directly tied to your manager's success. By understanding what they are trying to achieve, you'll be able to see how your work ties into the bigger picture and do a better job prioritizing your own goals.

When you get to know your manager and you are aware of their goals, you'll develop a new superpower: the ability to anticipate your manager's needs. I know, you can't read minds—at least, not yet—but with everything you learn about them and what you know about the company, you should be able to make educated guesses. The ability to provide your manager with what they need before they even think to ask you for it will get you into the employee hall of fame. Anticipating needs can manifest in different ways. At its core, it means being attentive and reading between the lines, in order to help your manager be more successful.

I used to create the first version of the quarterly report presentation for my manager. I put together a nicely designed template and plugged in the raw information, which made it easier for them to get the report done. That simple step helped my manager get through the report faster, and in return, I got an up-close and personal view of the strategic work my manager was doing.

More than anything else, successfully managing up means managing your own work, by prioritizing your work so it supports your manager's goals, focusing on making an impact, and over-delivering. When you do your job well, you save your manager time, and you give them peace of mind. Plus, your good work reflects on them as leaders and makes them look good in front of their own manager.

Managing up is a very proactive process. It's up to you to make it happen, but you can turn it into a more collaborative relationship by telling your manager how to best use your talents. When you provide your manager with some guidance, you make it easier for them to give you the kinds of responsibilities you want to take on, and you get opportunities to play to your strengths. Don't be afraid to have this conversation with your manager, because you will be doing them a favor. It's not always clear for your manager where each employee shines, so offering this information will keep them from guessing.

If you want to master the art of managing your manager, you'll need to get comfortable with having difficult conversations with them. Whether you want to give them feedback on their leadership style or tell them the team has too much on their plates, you need to approach that conversation with one objective in mind: being helpful. You don't want to insult your manager or make it seem like you are complaining, so make sure you position the conversation as an offer to help. Remember, it's not about you; it's about them. Think how you would want to hear what you are about to tell them, and apply some empathy. Think how to make the conversation more actionable for them. Focus on facts, and offer your insights and opinions, but try to keep your emotions out of the equation. Whenever possible, suggest a solution to the problem you are presenting and save your manager the trouble of trying to fix it themselves. As long as you are direct, honest, and helpful, even the hardest conversation could turn into a positive step forward.

I remember a time when one of my employees pulled me aside and told me I wasn't doing a great job as a leader. We were rushing to get a campaign out on time, so instead of sharing feedback and allowing them to redo their work, I fixed it for them. That action saved me time, but it kept them from understanding what they did wrong and took away their opportunity to learn. It is hard to believe, but the casual and light-hearted way that employees delivered their feedback actually made me smile.

"Hey, Maya, if you keep doing my work for me, how will I ever learn how to do it myself? Maybe you could share some feedback instead? I'll make sure we don't have any setbacks."

I didn't enjoy hearing that criticism, but I appreciated it and I learned from it. Great managers know you are helping them see what they have missed when you share feedback, and they'll appreciate it. I never fixed anyone's work for them again and I know it made me a better leader.

Last but not least, successfully managing up relies on your ability to serve as an extension to your manager. You need to be their eyes and ears on the ground, because they can't be everywhere at the same time. It's up to you to notice problems, report incidents, or provide insights on conversations your manager isn't privy to. It's up to you to make sure they are never blindsided or surprised with something you already know. I'm not suggesting that you share gossip or spy on your colleagues. The focus should be on information that affects their ability to do their job well. Think about what I did for Google when I brought it to the manager's attention that their team had some communications problems that were affecting their work. I helped the manager address a problem early on, before it escalated, because I could see something they were not aware of.

Managing up is an ongoing process, so it is imperative that you keep an open line of communication with your manager. The better you get at managing your manager, the more projects and responsibilities you will be trusted with, until eventually, you'll have the freedom to act almost completely independently. That is the end goal of managing up: gaining autonomy and trust so you can focus on creating opportunities for yourself and delivering remarkable results.

Managing Across

To succeed in an organization, you need resources, information, and expertise from people across the company.

Managing across the organization tests your ability to build trust and to influence your colleagues with little or no organizational power. It is an indication of your ability to work well with people at all levels—across silos—who have different personalities.

Mobilizing your peers can't happen through email. You will need to walk the halls, get out of the office, share ideas with colleagues, listen to their concerns, and work together to accomplish mutual goals. But here is the challenge: when you're operating outside clear reporting lines, your colleagues may not immediately see why they should collaborate with you. That's when your influence superpowers come into play. You'll use your ability to craft a compelling narrative to present a mutually beneficial solution that makes sense for everyone.

The first step to crafting that narrative is to find a meaningful common purpose for you and your colleague. Once again, it all starts with getting to know your peers and learning about their viewpoints and goals. Knowing where they are coming from, what they are looking to achieve, and what motivates them could help you avoid roadblocks and help you find better solutions.

A best practice I learned from one of my employees is to spend my first month getting to know everyone at the company (or the business unit). I recommend scheduling lunch dates or casual conversations that are not business related. I found that kicking off the relationship with an agenda-free conversation allows both sides to focus on getting to know each other on a personal level.

Next, you want to establish credibility, by showcasing your expertise. Whether it's demonstrating that you can make well-informed decisions or that you have a history of delivering outstanding results, your goal is to get your colleagues to trust your experience and believe you know your stuff. Be subtle and keep it to a humble brag, because you do not want to come off as condescending (been there, done that). You can do that by helping your colleagues and demonstrating that you can work in the best interests of others, not just your own.

This sounds like fairly simple advice, but I managed to totally mess this one up. When I was the VP of Marketing at Colu, I had to work very closely with the Head of Design. She was an early employee at the company and helped build the product from its inception. She made every design, marketing, and brand decision in the absence of a marketing leader, and then one day, I joined the company and everything changed.

I was a new executive with a chip on my shoulder and a goal to make a big impact right away. I assumed all marketing responsibilities should immediately fall under my supervision, without taking into account the person who held the fort down prior to my arrival. Instead of listening and asking questions, I stormed in and took over. You can imagine how well that turned out. It was a disaster.

For weeks, the Head of Design and I butted heads and argued about every decision. It was so bad that the CEO eventually pulled me aside and told me I needed to figure out how to fix the relationship and make it work. I was embarrassed and wasn't sure what to do. I always got along well with my colleagues and was able to lead without authority, so I wasn't sure what I had done wrong this time around.

A close friend helped me see things more clearly. I wasn't leading anyone; I was trying to tell people what to do. That is not how you influence people. The Head of Design wasn't reporting to me directly, so it was up to me to convince her to work together, not bully her into it.

I invited her for coffee outside of the office, hoping that we could have an honest conversation.

It was so weird. We sat across the table from one another in silence. We both knew we needed to talk, and we both wanted to avoid that conversation more than anything. It was like going on a date, knowing that your boyfriend is going to break up with you, so you do everything in your power to avoid the real conversation. It was really awkward and tense for a while. Then, the most unexpected thing happened. The Head of Design started laughing—a good, deep laugh. I couldn't figure out what was so funny. Suddenly, I couldn't help myself and started laughing as well.

It was such a relief. Finally, we were both able to let our guards down and have an honest conversation. We decided to take turns and tell each other everything that we were thinking and feeling. I learned that she felt as though I didn't respect her, and that I wasn't sharing feedback in a constructive way. I told her that she was very quick to dismiss my suggestions, and that she kept making decisions about design without including me.

We kept going back and forth, until we ran out of bad things to say. Then, we started saying good things. I won't tell you that we became the best of friends afterward, but we established a few ground rules and an open line of communication. I learned what was important to her and how she preferred to get feedback, and she learned how her work impacted my ability to deliver results as an executive.

Clearly, if we had a conversation about our goals and got to know each other personally early on, we could have avoided many painful experiences.

Once you get to know your colleagues, you can start thinking about aligning your goals with theirs, or better yet, finding a way to frame your goals on a common ground. Just like with the influence formula, you want to make it about them and show your colleagues what they stand to gain by helping you and collaborating on a project. As much as I want to think people volunteer to help out based on the kindness of their heart, the reality is that a little incentive goes a long way.

After we established our ground rules, I had to share feedback with the Head of Design. I had to ask her to make changes to a website page she created and basically start over. I knew sharing my opinion, even though it was based on a decade of experience, wouldn't be enough to convince her the page needed an upgrade to perform better. As far as she was concerned, it was a beautifully-designed website page. I decided to wait two weeks before reaching out, so I could get data that showed how poorly the website was converting.

Instead of starting the conversation with my request for changes, I started by offering to share the data with her, to show her how the website page she built was performing. The Head of Design was surprised by my suggestion, but she seemed excited to learn how and where her work was delivering an impact. I logged in to the Google Analytics account and walked her through every metric. I showed her where we had drops in conversion, which was the problem I was trying to solve. Together, we came up with ideas on how to improve the user experience.

That conversation took an hour, which was way more than what it would have taken for me to simply ask for the changes I wanted, but it was worth it, because two amazing things happened afterward.

First, the Head of Design was motivated and even excited to work on the changes, because she was included in the process and could see the value in improving the website conversion.

The second thing that happened was that she started tracking the impact of everything she designed. She didn't wait for me to show her the data again; she checked it herself, then worked to constantly optimize the impact of her work.

The way you frame your message and explain your position is important. You need to meet people where they are and gradually lead them towards the conclusion you want them to make. I could have told the Head of Design exactly what changes were needed to support my website conversion goals, but that wouldn't have been motivating; it would have been antagonizing.

In order to influence people without authority, you need to make sure you serve their best interests as well as yours. You need to make sure both you and your peers have skin in the game. In the words of Cuba Gooding Jr., you want to help them help you. If it sounds familiar, you are right. You learned how to do all that in Chapter 6, when we discussed the influence formula.

Whether you are managing up or across, the key to leading without authority is to remember it's a long-term process, not an on/off switch. Gaining trust and building relationships takes time, but it is an invaluable tool for your career.

Get to know the people you work with, put their best interest ahead of yours, and craft a mutually beneficial narrative. You'll be amazed with what you can achieve when you take this approach.

Chapter 7 Checklist and Summary

Managing up:
- ❏ Get to know your manager
- ❏ Understand their goals
- ❏ Learn to anticipate their needs
- ❏ Manage your own work
- ❏ Tell your manager how to use your talent
- ❏ Be your manager's eyes and ears
- ❏ Learn how to have difficult conversations

Managing across:
- ❏ Get to know your colleagues and build relationships with them
- ❏ Learn what drives them and what they care about
- ❏ Gain credibility
- ❏ Find some common ground
- ❏ Craft a compelling story with a positive outcome for them
- ❏ Align expectations

Chapter 8
Skill #8—Extreme Accountability

When I was 18, I joined the army. Just a few months after graduating high school, I packed a few of my belongings and left home. In Israel, where I was born and raised, military service is mandatory. At the age of 18, men and women are enlisted to serve their country for a few years.

I was stationed in a closed base, which meant I couldn't come and go as I pleased. Every other week, I got to go home for a short weekend, but I had to earn that right by passing the weekly inspection. As a soldier, I was expected to keep my quarters neat and clean. It is such an imperative aspect of the training, they actually teach you how to make your bed at boot camp, and they are quite strict about it. Every Friday morning, the base sergeant would perform an inspection of our quarters, to make sure we were keeping them spotless. The inspection included our dorms as well as the shared facilities like our bathrooms, showers, and a small yard.

I remember how nervous I was before my first inspection. The beds were made, personal belongings were tucked away neatly in the closet, the floors were mopped, and the room smelled of disinfectant. I was confident we would pass with flying colors.

The sergeant and his assistant walked in and took a quick look. The sergeant headed straight to the window and ran his fingers along the sill. I stopped breathing. He looked at his finger for a short while and then moved on to the next room. The entire room sighed in relief. It was clean.

A few seconds later, the sergeant was already on his way to the second floor and we started to pack our bags for the weekend.

A sharp call stopped us dead in our spot. We were being called out to the yard by the sergeant. That was not a good sign.

More than a hundred women walked out quickly and formed straight lines in the yard, in anticipation of the bad news. As it turned out, we all failed the inspection miserably.

The rooms were clean, but the common areas were far from it. You see, we were all too busy thinking about our own rooms that no one paid attention to the shared facilities. They were left unattended and the sergeant was not happy. He reminded us that the common areas were a shared responsibility, so he held *all of us* accountable for the results. We all failed.

Even in your early training, the army teaches you to be accountable to more than just yourself. One of the first things you learn is how to be accountable for the people you serve with. When we failed to practice that accountability, the sergeant decided to teach us a lesson.

My heart sunk. I was really looking forward to going home and meeting my family. I didn't want to spend the weekend stuck in the base. Why didn't I think about the common areas? Why didn't anyone else clean them? What a stupid mistake!

More than 100 women were grounded to the base for four hours because no one took responsibility for the common area. It wasn't anyone's fault; it was everyone's fault.

Luckily, the sergeant decided to cut us some slack. He set up a second inspection for later that day, to give us another chance to get our weekend pass.

That was one of my first encounters with accountability and it taught me a lesson: accountability is not just about what you commit to doing yourself, it's also about your commitment to your team, your colleagues, and the people you share a bathroom with.

Accountability is a term that gets thrown around a lot, so let's define it, for the context of this book.

Accountability is an internal commitment or willingness to take ownership, accept responsibility, and follow through on what you promised yourself and others that you would do. Accountable people are committed to generating the best results for themselves, their colleagues, and the company—even when it gets hard or inconvenient. Your personal commitment is often referred to as taking ownership and it is internally-focused. The commitment to others is externally-focused and reflects your ability to put the greater good ahead of your own interests.

Accountability is a mindset and a belief that informs your decision-making and drives the actions you take to achieve success in everything that you do. Accountability isn't something that can be forced on you. It is something you decide to learn and practice.

But what does it mean to be accountable in the workplace, as an employee?

Accountability at work is about showing up and taking initiative. It means you don't just do your job; you step up to make sure you do what is right for the company. People who are accountable at work strive to deliver successful outcomes, no matter what it takes. They fight through any and all challenges to get results, regardless of politics or seniority, without assigning blame or complaining. People who are accountable think of the bigger picture and focus on delivering the best possible results for the business, not just for themselves. They collaborate, help others, and find new ways to get things done.

Last but not least, people who are accountable accept their responsibility and own it. "It's not my fault" is not something they ever say. They admit their mistakes and take steps to learn and improve.

Accountability is not exactly the same as responsibility. People who are responsible do what they are told to do in the time frame they are allotted, but that doesn't mean they do a good job. Let me give you an example, to explain the difference.

A responsible employee will be given a task to write and publish a piece of content, and they'll do it, no questions asked. An accountable employee will be given the same task, but they'll realize the topic is all wrong for the target audience. They'll know there is a better way to get the results the company is aiming for. They'll do the research to find a better topic for their audience. Then, they will create a more relevant and valuable article, in the time frame that was given, because what matters to them is the end result. They are accountable for the outcomes, not just the process of getting things done. They are ready to go above and beyond, to make sure their work has the biggest possible impact.

Being responsible is important and it is table stakes in the workplace. Being accountable is what makes you an invaluable employee.

How can you cultivate accountability?

Accountability is not a trait you are born with. It is a skill you develop throughout your life. In order to start a conversation on how to become more accountable, we first have to talk about our belief systems and their potential to fuel our behavior and predict our success. There are two beliefs that make up the foundation of accountable thinking and we are going to review them both.

The first belief is referred to in science as "locus of control."

Locus of control is the degree to which people believe that they have control over the outcome of events in their lives. People can have an internal or an external locus of control, depending on what they believe to be true about themselves.

As the environment around you changes, what do you attribute success and failure to—things you have control over, or to forces outside your influence?

If you believe that you have control over your life, such as the power and the ability to influence events, and if you believe things don't just happen but you have an active part in making them happen, then you have an internal locus of control. People who develop an internal locus of control believe that they are responsible for their own success. On the opposite end, those with an external locus of control believe that external forces, such as other people, the circumstances, or luck determine their outcomes.

Having an internal locus of control is imperative in the process of developing accountability. If you don't believe you have the power to drive change, the idea of change will never cross your mind. You'll let things run their course and hope for the best, instead of owning up and taking action. People who are accountable adopt an internal locus of control and believe their actions create their destiny. This belief in their ability to make a difference allows them to challenge the status quo, ask the right questions, and dare to come up with ideas for improvement.

Here is the thing, though, locus of control comes into play in every aspect of our lives, not just at work. Think about a student who failed an exam. If they have an internal locus of control, they'll blame themselves. They'll think they didn't put in enough time and effort to study and they will do everything in their power to do better, the next time around. A student with an external locus of control will blame the teacher, the exam, or their dumb luck.

In a similar way, an employee who has an external locus of control and delivers mediocre results at work will blame their manager, their company, or the economy for their inability to succeed. The problem is that people with an external locus of control think the outside world is what drives their success or failure at work, so they don't see the point of being accountable and doing whatever it takes to succeed.

By adopting an internal locus of control and believing effort and skills are the forces that drive success and failure, you can become more accountable.

The second belief that fuels accountable thinking is having a growth mindset. We touched on this topic earlier in Chapter 2, when we talked about becoming a lifelong learner, but now we can go deeper and explore how this belief can affect your ability to become accountable.

Having a growth mindset means you believe your personality and your traits can be developed through dedication and hard work. This means you acknowledge that you can grow and learn, as an individual and as a professional. You understand you were not born with all the traits and skills you could ever have, so you invest in improving yourself.

On the opposite end, people with a fixed mindset assume that character, intelligence, and creative ability are predetermined traits that can't be changed in any meaningful way. They believe who they are right now is all they will ever be, so there is no need for them to broaden their horizons, develop curiosities, or try out new things.

It is important that you cultivate an internal locus of control and a growth mindset, if you want to become more accountable.

You must believe in your ability to learn and improve, in order to strive for success, and you must believe you have control over your life, in order to muster the courage to show up.

Let's start building your accountability muscle.

There are four ways you can build your accountability skills.

1: Train yourself to be unsatisfied with the status quo.

If you want to be open to change, you first need to have the ability to see things in a new light. You need to change your perspective, to re-imagine what is possible, and train yourself to ignore limitations. You need to aspire for more and assume there's always one more thing you can do. In order to aim higher, you need to cultivate the ability to be unsatisfied with the status quo, even if it means criticizing other people's work as well as your own. In this case, complacency is the biggest enemy of accountability. I'm not saying nothing you do will ever be good enough, but rather that you should hold the belief there are always ways to improve.

Give yourself credit for achievements, but then ask yourself: What's next? How can this be improved? Is this the best I/we can do?

2: Leave your ego at the door.

We've all been there. We want to make the right decision and we want to be selfless, but our egos pull us in the opposite direction. We know there is a better solution, but we are afraid to admit we were wrong—that we are tempted to protect our own reputation, at the expense of the company. We are driven by our desire to avoid pain, and that survival mechanism—our ego—clouds our judgment and stops us from being accountable. That means you won't be able to develop your accountability muscle without letting go of your ego. As an employee who wants to deliver exceptional results, you need to shift your focus from your own wants and needs to what would be the most beneficial for the company.

Here is how you can train yourself to let go of your ego:

1) **Make a decision, as the person you want to be.**—
   I have a vision of the person I want to be in 10 years. "Future me" is better, smarter, more experienced, and

nearly perfect. I try to make my decisions *now* as if I already was that future version of myself because it helps me eliminate the fear of making a mistake. "Future me" doesn't need to optimize for her own benefit, so I trust that she would do what is best for the company.

2) **Ask yourself: What would my idol do?**—I'm going to share a secret with you. I have a professional crush on Dave Gerhardt. He is one of the most inspiring marketers in my industry right now and I'm obsessed with his content. I am telling you this because every time I need to make tough decisions, I ask myself "What would DG do?" This frame of reference helps me detach myself from the situation and make a more neutral decision. If you are thinking this method sounds exactly like the first one, you are absolutely right. It's all about shifting perspective. Some people find it hard to imagine their future self, but they can easily identify with someone they look up to.

3) **Take yourself out of the equation.**—We've already established that being an accountable employee means you optimize for the best outcomes. If you want to make fewer biased decisions, start with the business in mind. Ask yourself what is best for the company, not for you. This is a hard one, because you'll have to admit you are factoring your own best interests into your decisions. There's no shame in that. Trust me when I say our brain has incredible ways to justify just about anything, if it's for our personal benefit. If you approach the situation by admitting your perspective is skewed, you can look for those biases and eliminate them.

3: Practice team accountability.

Being accountable for yourself is hard, but being accountable for others takes this practice to a whole new level.

By practicing team accountability, you will essentially take on group responsibilities and make them your own. You will be the person who stands up in the yard and declares they are going to clean the bathroom and asks for volunteers. You will be the person who makes sure the team gets the job done, even if you have to do the heavy lifting yourself. You will be the person who motivates everyone to keep going when it gets hard, by reminding everyone why they are doing what they are doing in the first place.

Being the person who can rally the troops and lead by example is a leadership quality that stems from accountability and a devotion to the task.

Volunteer, stand up (even if you want to hide in the corner), take on the job no one wants to do, and lead by example.

4: Own up to your mistakes.

No one wants to admit they are wrong. It hurts to admit you made a mistake, but accountable people do not hide behind excuses. They don't avoid the hard questions, they do not shift blame, and they don't deflect. They own up to their mistakes, they assume responsibility, and they take action to make sure they do not repeat that mistake.

You can't take credit when you are doing well and run away when you screw up. Being accountable means you take full responsibility, whether the outcome is good or bad.

Advanced reading: What is extreme accountability? How can you use it?

This is a hard one to swallow. I had trouble accepting this concept when I first heard about it, so brace yourself.

Extreme accountability means you believe that everything that happens to you is your fault. E-V-E-R-Y-T-H-I-N-G.

It's a controversial concept, to say the least, but the philosophy behind this idea is quite simple. If you believe you are accountable for everything that happens to you (good or bad), you have control over every result you produce in life.

You may be thinking to yourself that this actually makes sense. I mean, you already believe you are responsible for your own actions, but let me explain why this is so controversial. "Everything is your fault" doesn't refer to *what you do*; it refers to everything that *happens to you*.

For example (and this is the extreme version), if a piano fell from the 10th floor of a building and crushed your car, it would be your fault.

The good news is that if everything is your fault, then every good thing that happened in your life, no matter how much it seemed like luck or coincidence, is your doing.

I choose to embrace the good and the bad about this concept, because I find that training myself to think in extremes resonates deeply and reminds me I have the power to change my life.

I use this controversial thought as a motivational force. In the bad times, it empowers me to make a change, and in the good times, it makes me proud.

You can use this concept, to develop your own accountability, by constantly reminding yourself that it's your fault. Instead of blaming someone else, even though you REALLY think it's their fault, own up to it, and take responsibility. Use the power of "everything is my fault" to motivate you to do better.

When I was leading marketing at Colu, I had to work closely with the product team to coordinate launch campaigns for new product features. I had access to the product roadmap and I was included in email conversations that reviewed the launch timeline. However, somehow, I ended up launching a campaign without a feature.

I relied on a schedule I had been given a few weeks earlier and developed a campaign accordingly. No one told me the schedule had changed, so I did my job and launched the campaign.

It was an embarrassing experience. I sent an email to the entire company announcing the launch, and got an immediate response from the Product Manager, who let me know I had made a mistake.

I made a mistake? I shouted, inside my head. *Me? Why didn't you tell me the schedule had changed?*

After my initial rage subdued, I took a deep breath and re-evaluated the situation. I realized the whole thing was my fault. I didn't double-check the date. I didn't give the product team a heads up about the campaign, and I didn't go into the product to verify the feature was up and running before announcing it to the world.

Even though on paper, I did my job (I designed and launched a campaign based on the information I had), it was my fault. I know it sounds weird, but I was relieved. Once I realized what I could have done differently, I felt empowered. I knew it would never happen again, no matter who I would be working with.

That incident allowed me to build a better process for launch campaigns and taught me to be a better communicator.

You can't blame others, but you also can't blame the circumstances, luck, or the world.

Blame-shifting is a bad habit. It essentially means you have no control and you let life happen to you. Someone else got that promotion? *I guess it's because your manager is an idiot.* You screwed up an assignment? *It's because the IT team didn't renew your software license.* You are living paycheck to paycheck? *It's the economy, stupid!*

Now, I get it. Sometimes, we need someone to blame. We need to vent or blow off some steam, to make it easier to deal with difficult or disappointing situations. I'm with you. When things don't go according to plan, I spend hours thinking, rethinking, and over-analyzing. My husband will testify to that; he has to endure such conversations all the time.

The big difference is that I use the process of introspection to complain privately *and* to find a solution. No matter how the conversation starts, it always ends up with what I can do to change the situation or do better next time. Usually, halfway through my rant, I realize it's all my fault and I shift my focus to finding a solution. That is what works for me.

You may need to write things down, to get your thoughts on paper. Some people work out or go for a run, to clear their heads and reboot. Find what works for you and remind yourself it is all your fault. It will help you build your accountability muscle.

Chapter 8 Checklist and Summary

How to develop accountability:
- ❏ Learn to be unsatisfied with the status quo
- ❏ Leave your ego at the door
    - ✓ Make a decision about the person you want to be
    - ✓ Ask yourself: What would my idol do?
    - ✓ Take yourself out of the equation
- ❏ Practice team accountability
- ❏ Own up to your mistakes

How to handle extreme accountability:
- ❏ Remind yourself that everything is your fault
- ❏ Avoid blame-shifting
- ❏ Go through the process of introspection
- ❏ Come up with solutions or ways to improve

Chapter 9
Skill #9—Become a Planner

You may not know this about me, but I'm a planner. I have a spreadsheet for everything in my life, including my career. I learned early on it's important to identify a destination and set a course for your career and your success. Otherwise, you get lost.

Think about it this way: when you want to get from one place to another, you choose the destination on your GPS. You don't wander the streets, hoping you'll get to where you want to go. That would be crazy, right? Unfortunately, when it comes to their careers, many people forget to set their destination and end up spending their careers wandering around.

If you know where you want to be in a few years, you can actively work on getting there. I didn't get from an entry level position to VP by accident. My 10 promotions in 15 years weren't just about hard work. I had a plan, for every step of the way. I set up career goals every year, to challenge myself and to make sure my focus was on what mattered the most for my career.

If you haven't had the opportunity to create a career roadmap before, you are in for a treat. We are going to create a step-by-step plan, with actionable tasks you can execute year-round, to grow your career.

A career roadmap is a strategic plan that helps you identify what to focus on and how to develop the skills you need to get to the next level in your career. When you have a clear goal, weekly actionable tasks, and a way to track your progress, you are 10 times more likely to follow through and actually work on your career development.

A roadmap can be flexible. To get started, you don't have to know where you want to be in a decade. You can start with the next job and take it from there, as you grow and learn. The important part is to have a plan to guide you.

Technically speaking, you can just go to work every day, do your job, and if you are lucky, or your stars align, you may get a promotion. But why take the chance? Why not plan in advance and make sure that you do?

If you are perfectly happy in your job and you want to keep doing it for the next decade, by all means, step away from the spreadsheet! Maybe this isn't the right season for you to make changes. However, if you are ready for more and if you want to skyrocket your career, you need a career roadmap.

Developing a career roadmap might sound like a lot of work—and it *will* require some effort—but it can be a fun and exciting experience. Yes, planning your future and envisioning the possibilities is something I consider to be fun.

A career roadmap is comprised of a few elements:
1) The destination—your career goal or dream job
2) The path—the career stepping stones that could lead you to your destination
3) The fuel in your tank—the skills you'll need to acquire, the knowledge you'll need to gain, and the experience you'll need to have to make it to the next level
4) The accelerator (putting the pedal to the metal)—the actions you'll need to take, the opportunities you'll need to create and seize, and the tasks you'll need to perform to move forward.

Building a career roadmap and being intentional about growing as a professional is an ongoing process. Some of these elements will require constant updating, and some could lead you for years. A lot of the heavy lifting happens at the beginning (when you work on setting your destination), but once you have a plan, it's mostly about following through and executing it.

It is best to use a document for the planning and a spreadsheet for the execution. I do that because I find it easier to separate the strategy from the day-to-day work. This way, I don't find myself staring at big audacious goals that freak me out every time I work on my tasks. When I use the spreadsheet to track progress, my viewpoint is limited to the few tasks I have outlined for the next week or month.

Choose what works for you, but make sure you write it down. If it's only in your head, it's not an actionable plan; it's just wishful thinking.

Step #1: Define Your Destination

I can't emphasize enough how important it is to have a well-defined destination. Without it, you won't have a valuable roadmap.

Your destination doesn't have to represent your entire career; it can highlight where you want to be in one, three, or five years. It's really up to you. If you already know where you want to be in a decade, go for it! If you are still exploring and experimenting, focus on the next job you want to have.

If you are not exactly sure where you want to go next, the following exercises could help you figure it out.

Exercise 1: The Perfect Day

The "Perfect Day" is a visualization exercise. It's a really simple and intuitive way to try and tap into what your future could look like.

To get the most out of this exercise, I recommend blocking off some time on your calendar and going somewhere quiet. You want to be in a good state of mind and away from distractions for about 30 minutes. (I like sitting in a noisy cafe with my headphones blasting songs from my favorite playlist. It helps me get in the right mood and ignore any and all distractions.)

When you are ready to get started, close your eyes and imagine what your perfect day would look like 10 years from now. Start from the moment you wake up in the morning. Where are you? Who are you with? What does your morning routine look like? Where do you work? How do you get to work? What does the office look like, if you have one? What do you do when you arrive? Who do you meet with throughout the day?

Imagine every little detail and let yourself get excited. Remember, you are thinking 10 years ahead, so anything is possible. You can be anything and anyone you want to be!

After you are able to vividly see and feel everything, open your eyes and start writing. Write everything that comes to mind. Don't censor yourself simply because something you imagined seems impossible. Write the career story of your dreams and own it. Don't be afraid to imagine who you could become. Let your imagination go wild and surprise yourself.

The whole thing should take you 20-30 minutes and you will end up with a story that outlines what you want to do and how you want to live. This is the first step to making everything—yes, *everything*—on that piece of paper come true.

Look at the story you wrote and start extracting insights. What was the profession you imagined? Did you have a specific role? What were you actually doing?

Create a bullet list of insights that could be used to better define your career destination.

When I went through this exercise, I imagined myself as the CMO of a Silicon Valley startup. I was leading a team and had the opportunity to make an impact on the company as one of the senior executives. In the career story I envisioned, I spent the first part of my day with my team—removing obstacles and solving problems. I participated in strategic discussions with management and had lunch with a colleague, to expand my network. The second part of my day was dedicated to marketing work and tasks I was personally responsible for: planning, tracking, strategizing, and creative thinking—all the things I absolutely love doing. In the evening, I would go home to have dinner with my husband and work on a personal project. At the time, it was a podcast about marketing. I could imagine what the office would look like and I knew what I'd be wearing, but more importantly, I could feel how I would feel when I had the career of my dreams—happy, proud, fulfilled, and energized.

When I wrote the story about my perfect day in 2013, I was nowhere near making it come true. I was not living in the United States, I wasn't in a leadership role, and I didn't have a podcast. However, none of that mattered. I just wrote about my dream; my vision of the person and the professional I wanted to become.

It's now seven years later, and I'm as close as I have ever been to realizing everything I have dreamed of. I live in San Francisco with my wonderful husband and I work as a startup consultant where I focus mostly on strategy, planning, and creative thinking. I had the opportunity to be the VP of Marketing for a fast-growing startup, where I led an incredible team and had a direct impact on the company's success. When it comes to my passion projects, I spent two years co-hosting a podcast about marketing with one of my dearest friends, who is a marketing genius, and now, I have a few new passion projects: writing and publishing a book (done!) and helping others achieve a new level of success.

Maybe you are not impressed. After all, seven years is a long time, but I had ambitious goals that required time, patience, and dedication to accomplish. I'm not sure where I'd be right now without my "perfect day" vision. The story I wrote stuck in my head and kept me going all of these years, especially when things got hard and frustrating.

If visualization isn't for you, maybe the next exercise could help.

Exercise 2: Use Mind Maps

Every time I felt stuck or unsatisfied in my career, I stopped to ask myself why. To really dig deep and understand what was causing me pain, I used a tool called a mind map. Mind mapping is a highly effective way of getting information in and out of your brain. It is a creative and logical process that literally "maps out" your ideas.

The objective of a mind map is to clearly visualize all your thoughts around a main topic.

Mind maps have a main element—usually represented as a circle in the middle of a page—and branches, which represent the ideas and details supporting that main element. (It kind of looks like a drawing of the sun.)

In order to define your dream job, you first need to outline everything you have done or are currently doing at your job, to get a clear view of your responsibilities and capabilities.

Start by taking a blank sheet of paper, drawing a circle in the middle, and writing your current job title or profession (for example: Marketing Operations Manager) in the circle.

Next, draw a line from the circle outwards. At the end of the branch, write down a responsibility or task that relates to your job. (For example, if you are a Marketing Operations Manager, one of your branches would say "design processes for executional excellence," and another could say "analytical skills.") Try to get at least 25 branches coming out of the center. You can include information from your current role or go broader and include information from every role you had to date.

Now that you have an overview of your experience, it's time to assess what you like and don't like doing at work. By clearly defining what you are passionate about and want to do more of (and what you prefer to avoid), you'll be able to put together a description for your dream job.

Simply divide your branches into two lists: things you like doing at work, and things you don't. When you are done outlining your likes, add skills or responsibilities you aspire to learn. For example, you may want to become a manager, so you'll add leadership to the list of things you like to do at work.

The idea behind this exercise is to help you find a new role that encapsulates what you love doing and excludes most of what you hate. By starting with outlining the things you love doing instead of committing to a specific role, you are allowing yourself to come up with new ideas for roles you may never consider otherwise.

When your list of likes is complete, it's time to find a job description that encapsulates everything you love and excludes the things you hate doing.

If you are not sure what type of roles could allow you to focus on what makes you happy, I suggest doing some research on LinkedIn.

LinkedIn can be a great resource when you are trying to identify roles that include specific skills. You can discover interesting roles by searching LinkedIn for job postings that include the keywords you have outlined. You may come across positions you didn't consider before. For example, if you love talking to customers, you could search for "customers" and discover roles like "customer success," "customer support," and "customer marketing," to name a few. When you identify a role that interests you, look for job postings with the same title, to learn what the role entails. You want to make sure it includes many of your likes.

Next, search for these job titles under "people" and LinkedIn will surface professionals who are currently occupying these roles.

If you click to see the profiles of the individuals that surfaced, you'll be able to learn a bit more about what they do and what they are responsible for. Once you find a role that seems interesting, go on and find a few more professionals with that same title, to give you a broader view of the role. I highly recommend reaching out to a few of those professionals and talking to them, too, because there is nothing like firsthand experience to help you understand if that role could be a good fit for you.

When you have a few potential roles that would include a lot of what you love doing, make sure they don't come with too many of the things you hate. Narrow down your list and pick one or two possible roles. Write the names of those roles in the middle of your mind map, because they are your career destinations.

Whether it's your next role or your dream job 10 years from now, once you have a clearly articulated destination, you can start the journey to turn your story into a reality.

Step #2: Outline the Path

After you've identified your dream job and where you want to go, it is time to return to reality and create a plan that could take you there.

There are different ways to get to your destination and the path may change as you grow and learn—as both a professional and an individual. You may start with one specific route in mind and hit a wall or just realize there's a better way, so don't get too attached to the path. Remember, it is just a means to an end.

How can you outline the path to your destination?

- You can start with a few educated guesses. If you have been in an industry or profession for a while, you might know what the ladder looks like. For example, if you are a Customer Support Manager (CSM), the next step could be Senior Manager. Write down your assumptions and then validate them with some light detective work.
- Ask colleagues or friends for their perspective. Alternatively, talk to managers or senior executives at your company. They could be great resources to learn from, regarding career development. If your immediate contacts aren't helpful, you could go back to LinkedIn to find clues.

When I started planning my path to a CMO role, I wanted to know what it was going to take to get from where I was at the time to my dream job.

Marketing is a broad profession with multiple specialties and I wasn't sure if one specialty would be more valuable than the others, so I decided to do some stalking. I searched LinkedIn for CMOs in Silicon Valley who were leading marketing for tech startups. I clicked through to their individual profiles and looked at their career paths. I focused on the last two or three roles they had before becoming CMOs and looked for trends. Was there a specific specialty they all shared? Did they all have the same paths or different ones? I summarize my findings in a spreadsheet, so I could track the trends.

I know that sounds a bit over the top, but I found out the CMOs I tracked had different career paths and diverse experiences. Some grew with the companies they worked for and some made a jump from a previous role to the C-suite. It seemed like they came from different backgrounds but when I crunched the numbers, I saw that the majority of CMOs came from two disciplines: Demand Generation and Product Marketing.

Technically speaking, my research found fewer marketers who made it to the C-suite with a communications and PR background. That was an important insight. I originally thought it didn't matter what marketing role I took on, as long as I kept taking more senior roles, but the process of outlining my path helped me realize that wasn't the case. My research wasn't statistically valid, but it gave me a direction. Later on, I spoke to a few of these professionals and was able to validate my assumptions.

By reviewing LinkedIn profiles of professionals who made it to your destination, you can map out a few possible routes that could get you from where you are today to your destination. Better yet, you can reach out to those professionals and ask them about their path and the decisions they made along the way.

- Map out a few possible routes based on the information you collected and prioritize your options. You can rank them by their probability, difficulty to achieve, or by what sounds like the most exciting and fun path to take.
- Focus on your top two options.

I ended up outlining two different routes to get to my dream job. I could take a Product Marketing role at a bigger company where I could grow into the CMO role, or aim for a startup where I could lead marketing in an executive role, even though the company would be much smaller.

Narrowing down the options helped me focus on the roles that could lead me to my destination. It helped me say no to the wrong opportunities and avoid wasting time on shiny titles that could have been lucrative in terms of compensation but useless when it came to driving my career forward.

At the end of Steps #1 and #2, you should know what your dream role is, and what the types of jobs that could lead you there are. Whether you are one step away from your dream or three, knowing what the next step looks like will help you take action right now, to get to where you want to be tomorrow.

Step #3: Check Your Fuel Levels

Now that you know where you are going because you mapped out a route, it's time to figure out what it's going to take to get there. This step is all about identifying gaps and what you are going to have to learn, achieve, or experience to close those gaps and become the person you need to be to get your dream job.

Focus on identifying the most relevant gaps (the ones you'll need to close, to get your next job).

One of the simplest ways to do this is to go back and look at the job descriptions for the role you want. Those job descriptions will usually include a detailed explanation of the responsibilities you'll need to assume and the experience you will be expected to demonstrate. Requirements may differ from one company to another, but if you review more than a handful of job descriptions, I'm sure you'll be able to identify some commonalities.

Remember the LinkedIn research you did to find your path? You are going to stalk these professionals for a bit longer. Those professionals can tell you exactly what it took to get to where they are today because they actually did it. They can outline every skill and every experience you will need to work on to get in their shoes, so reach out to them. If you are not sure how to get people to accept your invitation on LinkedIn, go back to the chapter about adopting a learner's mindset where I outline how to reach out to influencers. The principles are exactly the same.

- Summarize the information you collect from your conversations with those professionals, as bullet points. Outline the skills and types of experiences you will need to gain. For example, you may need leadership skills for the next level, or a great understanding of business analytics. Maybe it's about getting more experience working directly with customers, or maybe you need to get certified using a specific platform.

- Rate your list from the most important to the least important skill (where most important means you must master that skill in order to get the job you want and the least important means it would be a nice addition, but you may succeed without it).

- Next, rate yourself on every skill, to determine how well you qualify. For example, if the role requires management experience and you don't have any, give yourself a 0. If the role requires technical skills you have mastered, give yourself a 10. If the role requires great communications skills and you feel quite confident in your abilities, write 8, but if your communications skills are only decent, write 5.

- Highlight anything that was rated lower than an 8, with a focus on the intersection of skills that are crucial for the role and those you rated the lowest for, so you know the exact areas where you need to improve. Ideally, when you are done with this exercise, you'll have 3-5 bullet points that represent the biggest gaps you need to close.

- If you identify skills you already have, cross them off so you can focus on what you actually need to improve. Be honest with yourself about your current experience. This is between you and yourself—you don't need to impress anyone—so keep it real.

Step #4: Put the Pedal to the Metal

This is it. This is when it all gets real.

You have done all of the preparations. Now, it's time to do the work. Are you excited? You should be; this is where the magic happens! This step is going to transform your current reality into your future one.

It's time to ask yourself a very important question: *No bullshit, what is it going to take?*

You need to ask that question about every skill or experience gap you identified, in order to come up with ideas on how to gain those skills.

Here are a few examples to get you started:

1) **Learn on your own.**—There are so many ways to learn independently. Some examples include reading a book, taking a course, watching a YouTube video, or utilizing the growth machine from Chapter 2. If your gap can be filled by consuming information and it doesn't require a whole lot of doing to gain experience then just set aside time to learn.

2) **Find or create an opportunity at your current job.**—As you may recall, there's a whole chapter about creating opportunities at your current job to gain the experience you are missing (Chapter 4). You can ask for

more responsibilities, initiate projects, or volunteer to help other teams, to name a few.

3) **Just do it.**—If you are not able to find opportunities to learn a new skill at work for some reason, create your own project. Build a website, write a blog post, volunteer at a local store (for example, do their taxes for them), and/or create open source projects to test your coding skills. No matter what it is, just do it. This is a great way to gain experience if you are thinking about changing careers or taking on a new discipline. You get to experiment and gain relevant experience that your current employer can't offer.

When I started my podcast, I knew nothing about recording or editing audio, but after 15 episodes, I was an expert. Today, I could easily launch and edit a podcast for the companies I work for.

Another example is what one of my friends did when he wanted to get into social media. He was an avid gamer and his dream was to be a Community Manager for a gaming company. The problem was that he didn't have any formal experience. His career was focused on operations and not marketing. His solution was to reach out to one the biggest Facebook groups for gamers and offer to help them manage their community page for free.

So, he did.

After a short conversation, the team realized he was passionate about what they were doing and gladly accepted his offer. Six months later, he had hands-on experience and a network of potential customers.

Putting Theory into Practice: Make Your Steps Actionable, Track Your Progress, and Celebrate Your Wins

All of these ideas are great, but you need to make them actionable. You want to end up with specific, bite-sizes tactical actions you can take right now. These tasks need to be so clear that a stranger with no context about your goals could execute them.

A while back, I wanted to gain more public speaking experience. I knew this was something I had to do outside of work and I knew I had to find speaking opportunities. That's not a well-defined *action*. "Gaining more public speaking experience" is a *goal*.

This is what an action plan for this goal looked like:

- Find a topic for a keynote speech
- Outline the keynote speech
- Map out marketing events in San Francisco with 50-500 attendees
- Find the event organizers and their contact details
- Reach out to the event organizers and pitch the keynote idea
- Secure at least two speaking opportunities by August (three months)

You get the idea.

Start outlining specific actions that could help you achieve your goals so you can (1) avoid overwhelming yourself, and (2) acknowledge and track your progress. People tend to shut down when they are faced with a massive obstacle, so keep your action list in bite-sized pieces. It's hard to assess how well you are doing on a task that takes six months, but if you outline actions that can be executed in a few hours or days, you'll be able to track them and acknowledge your progress. Here, you can use a spreadsheet to help you set out your tasks in one column and track your progress in another. This process will result in a log of bite-sized, specific, actionable tasks you can choose from when you plan your week.

Next, plan out your weekly tasks. Set up time on your calendar to plan the week ahead and choose one or two tasks you can tackle, to make some progress toward your big goal. Block time on your calendar to work on these tasks throughout the week.

For my goal of gaining more public speaking experience, a good weekly task would be to map out marketing events in San Francisco with 50-500 people. It's very clear that I need to do a Google search, create an initial list, and then click through to the website of every event on that list, just to find out if it could be a good speaking opportunity.

Initially, it will probably feel like you are not making a lot of progress, but these tasks will have a compounding effect. You'll be amazed to see how far you've gone in just a few weeks!

Following these exact guidelines, I was able to secure my first speaking opportunity just a few weeks after I set up this goal. And once I had that experience, it was easier to get the next opportunities. I ended up speaking at five different events that year!

Celebrating success (even if it's small) will encourage you to stay the course. Take time to enjoy your journey and reward yourself by celebrating your accomplishments, regardless of how big or small they might be. Remember, some progress is still progress!

Execute, Execute, Execute

Your career roadmap is almost done! You now have a destination, you know what your next role should be, you know what it takes to get there and where you have gaps, and you have an action plan to gain the skills you need. Now, it's time to execute like crazy. Assuming you have more than one gap to cover, you'll need to decide what to focus on first.

You can tackle the biggest task or start with the easiest to gain momentum. (I like to work on one gap at a time and hammer out all the tasks related to that gap in a matter of weeks.) You may prefer to work on separate skills at the same time, to boost your creativity. Honestly, just stick to what works for you and keeps you going.

Here is what most people fail to realize: it is not hard to design the career of your dreams. It's a simple process anyone can go through. The challenge lies in the execution. Being consistent, doing the work, and not giving up halfway through will produce the results you desire.

Making progress is kind of like climbing a tower where all the way up, everything looks the same. When you look up, you see stairs. If you pause to look down, you see more stairs. It's only when you are able to spot the light from the top that you realize how far you have gone, even though you were climbing all along. Don't stop climbing!

Chapter 9 Checklist and Summary

How to create your career roadmap:

Step #1: Define your destination—your career goal or dream job
- ❏ Visualize and write out your perfect day
- ❏ Create a mind map of your current job
- ❏ Figure out what you want to do more of
- ❏ Identify your potential next role (use LinkedIn profiles and job descriptions)

Step #2: Outline the path—the career stepping stones that could lead you to your destination
- ❏ Search for professionals with your dream job
- ❏ Outline their path
- ❏ Identify common patterns
- ❏ Map out a few routes to your dream job destination

Step #3: The fuel in your tank—the skills you'll need to acquire, the knowledge you'll need to gain, and the experience you'll need to have to make it to the next level
- ❏ Find professionals who are doing the work you want to do
- ❏ Talk to them

- Review job descriptions for your dream role
- Identify gaps between who you are today and who you need to be
- Map out the skills you will need to acquire

Step #4: The accelerator (putting the pedal to the metal)—the actions you'll need to take, the opportunities you'll need to create and seize, and the tasks you'll need to perform to move forward.

- Turn every skill gap into a goal
- Brainstorm ideas on how to accomplish each goal
- Come up with actionable, bite-sized tasks that will help you achieve your goal
- Schedule time on your calendar to work on your tasks every week
- Track your progress
- Celebrate wins

Execute, to produce the results you desire, and don't stop climbing!

You can download the career roadmap toolkit at www.mayagrossman.com/resources.

Chapter 10
Skill #10—Develop the Habit of Tracking Your Success

The last time I wanted to update my LinkedIn profile, it took me about a week to gather a list of my achievements, and it was even harder to find the numbers to support my claims. It wasn't because I didn't have any achievements but because I didn't take the time to track them as they were happening! It was hard to try to remember every success I had when I hadn't taken the time to document them.

I found myself going through old emails and scraping social media channels I used to manage, in order to find the numbers to showcase my work. It was frustrating. I couldn't remember half of the things I'd done. The things I could remember still needed supporting evidence.

After going through this unpleasant experience, I swore I would never forget to document my success again, and to make this promise stick, I developed a simple tracking system.

Even if it is early in your career, you are expected to prove your professional aptitude with results, which are usually measured with numbers. I don't think you can get away with a resume that lists responsibilities anymore. You need to back up your claims for experience with achievements and results. Employers don't care that you "were responsible for office supplies," but that you were "able to negotiate with suppliers and reduce costs by 20%."

Tracking your success is as easy as updating a document once a month. As long as you turn it into a habit and update it regularly, you'll have an achievement reference list whenever you need it. It's a simple process that shouldn't take more than an hour of your time, but for some reason, it is not obvious that it should be part of your career development process.

Tracking your success has a few beneficial side effects. Constantly documenting success could help you feel more accomplished and give you a confidence boost. Looking at your list every other week could help you keep your achievements at the forefront of your mind, and make it easy to use them as examples in your everyday life. Plus, when you look back at something you've done, it can feel a lot smaller than it really is, especially as time goes by and your focus shifts to other things. Capturing success as it happens will help guarantee that you take into account every achievement—big or small.

Developing the habit of tracking your success and achievements will help you position yourself as an invaluable employee.

I didn't always track my achievements diligently. I had an a-ha moment, when I was first introduced to the Google resume. I couldn't believe that I hadn't done anything like that until now. I wondered how anyone could track and capture their success, if they weren't doing it on purpose. I then went and created my own version of the Google resume.

The original Google resume is a hub that captures employee responsibilities, programs, and achievements. Googlers create a Google resume when they want to be considered for a promotion, move to a different team, or just as a reference for their performance review. From what I observed, it's a common practice that is passed on from employee to employee, as a best practice.

I created a similar but upgraded, better version, and I advise creating such a spreadsheet for yourself, to track your success.

How to Use a Simple Spreadsheet to Track Your Success

Start a new spreadsheet and name the first 4 columns:

- Responsibilities
- Goals
- Achievements
- References

In the first column, outline the responsibilities you have in your current role and the ones you had in your past roles, just like on a resume. A responsibility could be "website management" or "strategy development."

For every responsibility area, outline the goals you will need to achieve and set qualitative and quantitative KPIs (Key Performance Indicators) to define what success looks like. For example, if your responsibility is website management, one of your goals could be to increase organic traffic by 10% or improve conversion rates from 3% to 12%.

The third column is for tracking your achievements. This column highlights your success in achieving your goals. For example, if your goal was to increase the website traffic, this column would include the actual results you were able to achieve. In this case, it would say: increased website traffic by 5%, from July to October (of whatever year).

The last column is for references and it can include links to dashboards or reports to provide solid evidence for your success.

When it's time to update your resume or write your career story, you will be happy that you took the time to capture this information. If you work for a company that runs performance reviews, this document will come in handy. It will also make your life easier when you write summary reports for your manager, to showcase your contributions to the project you worked on.

One additional benefit that can be attributed to this process is that it serves as an incentive to focus on outcomes, not outputs. When you constantly look at the column for achievements and see that it is empty, you feel obligated to produce results.

Tracking your achievements is a really simple habit that makes a huge difference. Don't ignore it just because it sounds simple. Put a reminder on your calendar to do this every other week, and keep doing it. Those small wins will compound and you'll end up with a pretty impressive resume that is based on your achievements, rather than having just a checklist of responsibilities.

Chapter 10 Checklist and Summary

Build a document to track your achievements:
- ☐ Column 1: Your list of responsibilities
- ☐ Column 2: Goals and KPIs for each responsibility area
- ☐ Column 3: Achievements (tracking)
- ☐ Column 4: References

Put a reminder on your calendar to update your tracking document every other week.

INVALUABLE

Summary: The Invaluable Mindset—How it All Comes Together

Congratulations! You are well on your way to becoming an invaluable employee!

You took the time to read this book and start practicing the 10 skills, and that puts you miles ahead of most employees, so give yourself credit for making it this far.

Only a handful of people take ownership of their career so they can make their dreams come true, and you are about to make that happen!

It's true, you now have the strategies and the tools you need to skyrocket your career and position yourself in the top 10% of the workforce. All you need to do is take action and start implementing what you have learned, in order to become an invaluable employee.

Whether you are a recent graduate, a young professional, or an industry veteran who is looking for their next role, you can be an invaluable employee. Your invaluableness may take different shapes at different stages of your career, but it will always lead to the same result: it will give you a competitive advantage—the ability to be successful in anything that you do—in your career, and in life.

The 10 skills are applicable at any stage of your career and in any profession—whether you are a marketing executive or a florist, as the next story clearly demonstrates.

I was discharged from the army after I completed two years of service. I was eager to take some time off and travel, but I didn't have enough saved up in my bank account to afford it. I was still living with my parents, so I had to get a job to save up for the big trip. I didn't have any professional experience at the time, so I was looking for an entry level job that paid fairly well and didn't require me to commute very far.

My parents' house was in the suburbs, where agriculture was dominating the business activity in the economy. I ended up taking a job at a nursery, where I was part assistant and part florist, which was a weird combination. I was working for a small family business that grew and sold flowers all over the country. The owners were an older couple who had put their whole life into their business and worked around the clock to keep the place running.

It wasn't exactly a glorious job, as you can probably imagine. We had a tiny office that could barely fit the three of us, a massive flower refrigerator, and a packing area that looked like an old barn, with working stations for the florists to assemble flower bouquets.

The whole place felt like it was left behind from another era. It was a bit old and crumbly but it had character, and it always smelled like fresh cut grass and lilacs.

I was hired to help with daily chores like getting the mail, filing invoices, sending fax messages to buyers, and providing services to the few local customers who came in to buy flowers every weekend.

In a matter of days, I realized I had a lot of free time. I was doing everything the job entailed, but it wasn't enough to cover a full day's work. I had to make a choice. Do I work slowly, take my time, and collect a paycheck for doing exactly what I was asked to do, or do I volunteer to do more and make the most out of my time?

I didn't even have to think about it.

I liked my job and I was fond of the older couple, so I wanted to help them and their business succeed. Also, I couldn't stand being idle. Even at a young age, I had a dislike for not making good use of my time. I was a doer, and doers don't rest on their laurels. Doers *do*.

I decided to help out with everything and anything that came up—sales calls, flower arrangements, and even cleaning the flower refrigerator. The latter was not an easy task—it was freezing!

I became friends with the family's accountant and helped them close the books every month, which is how I learned about revenue, taxes, and terms of payments, as well as how to use the accounting software.

I became a trusted employee. I was constantly given more responsibilities, more opportunities to manage financial transactions, and more work with customers.

Looking back, I can't believe how much I learned from this "temp" job that was only meant to help me save enough money for my trip.

Back then, I couldn't explain why I was so eager to do more, and why I was working 16- and 18-hour shifts during the holiday season, when demand was through the roof. Why I was de-thorning roses to the point that my palms started bleeding? I just didn't think there was another way. I didn't think anyone in my position would act differently. It was my first real job, but I thought of it as the most important job in the world. I was committed and I cared. I was developing my invaluableness.

I worked for the company for seven short months, but I was able to make a big impact—big enough to get a raise without asking for one, and a bonus when sales were up! And I got one more thing—something I never dreamed of. I secured a grant that doubled my savings!

Remember how I was living in the suburbs? Well, most young people moved to the city to work in tech, which meant there was a shortage of people who were willing to stick around and work in agriculture. It was so bad that the government ended up offering grants to employees who complete at least six months of work in the field. Flower farming was considered an agricultural line of work, but the business I worked for didn't tick all the boxes to qualify for the grant.

The couple I worked for knew I wanted the grant, so they took the time to make the necessary adjustments to their business registry, in order to qualify and allow me to apply for the grant. Yes, they went out of their way, spent time and money, and wrote me a recommendation—all so that I could apply for the grant!

They were great people. Maybe they would have done the same for anyone who worked for them, but I don't think that was the case. I think going above and beyond, thinking like an owner, and taking initiative—essentially, being invaluable—was what drove their act of kindness.

SUMMARY

I got the grant and ended up traveling in South America for six months, which was three months longer than I had originally planned, thanks to their generosity.

You see, anyone can become invaluable, but that doesn't mean it's easy. Mastering the 10 skills in this book is going to require practice—a lot of practice. If all you do is read this book and don't take action to execute the strategies presented, you won't get very far. Learning is great, but doing is what will eventually skyrocket your career. You need to "do" if you want to turn these skills into a career accelerator. I know it might feel like mastering these skills will require a lifetime, but I promise you, it won't. Mastery will happen faster than you can imagine because these skills have a compounding effect. Each skill you learn builds on the skills you previously developed, so it gets easier to adopt them and make progress.

Each of the skills are valuable on their own, but the real magic happens when you are able to make them work together. You start thinking with the invaluable mindset and it becomes your default *modus operandi*. When you reach that point, it will no longer be hard to think strategically, and it won't require much effort or attention; it will just be who you are, and how you think and operate. You'll know when you reach that point because it will be obvious to you and to everyone around you that you are an invaluable employee, team member, or manager.

I know you have the ability to do this. I've trained and coached employees and team members and helped them develop the skills I shared in this book. I saw them go through a transformation and grow their invaluableness, so I have no doubt you could do it, too.

You *can* become invaluable.

I can't help but feel excited for you. My goal with writing this book was to help people just like you lead successful and fulfilling careers—not make more money, not get fancy titles, but have a freaking awesome career. While money and titles are all great perks, they are nothing in comparison to feeling damn good about yourself. When you lead a fulfilling career and when you proactively make almost anything you dream of come true, you feel pretty good about yourself.

You are in complete control and you have the power to design the career of your dreams and make it a reality. No matter what anyone else tells you, *you* get to decide what your future could look like. You have the power to set the course for your journey and make sure you enjoy the ride! You have the tools and the strategies to succeed, under any circumstances, and to future-proof your career.

You already have what it takes to become invaluable. I hope you chose to read this book because you know you were meant for more and you know you could do better. There is no better time to get started than right now. I hope you know exactly what you are capable of and you just needed a gentle nudge in the right direction and a few words of advice from someone who has been through this journey.

I believe in you, so you better believe in yourself, too. I know you have the power to grow your invaluableness and turn it into your superpower, and I can't wait to see what you do next!

Thank You

To my mom and dad, who always had blind faith in my ability to do anything I set my mind to: thank you.

To my husband, Lior, for kicking my ass whenever I needed it: I couldn't have done it without you.

To my amazing family: thank you for the love and support you gave me (and continue to give me)—and for never calling me "crazy" to my face!

A special thank you to Noa Sagy, my sister-in-law, who sent me pictures of my niece every single day for two years (and counting). The daily "Leia moments" warm my heart and remind me what really matters.

When I think about this book and how it came to be, there is one person I have to call out first and potentially embarrass in this section: Zack Weisfeld, who was my manager at Microsoft.

I'm not sure he remembers this moment, but we were sitting in his office, having one of our regular one-on-one meetings, when he said something that really changed the way I see myself. It was a defining moment one can only appreciate in retrospect.

INVALUABLE

I asked Zack how he would describe me to a potential hiring manager (because I was interviewing for another role at Microsoft) and he said only one word.

"Exceptional."

That word was stuck in my head for four years, begging to become the first step in writing this book, until I finally gave up and started writing. Thank you for everything you taught me throughout the years. You have single-handedly ruined my chances of becoming a complacent employee. I can't think of a better gift!

To Jordan, Jackson, Hanako, and Courtney, my invaluable feedback group: your input, comments, and questions made this book 100 times better. Thank you for having the honesty and the courage to tell me when I sucked.

To Yacov Amsalem, Eliezer Amsalem, Alon Meisles, Hedva Nahume Avraham, Motti Peer, Ayelet Noff, Nirit Horowitz, Amos Meiri, and Dana Heller: thank you for your leadership, your mentorship, and above all, your friendship. This book could have been really boring if I didn't have all these crazy stories and character-building experiences during our time together. I'm the manager I am today because you taught me well and always held me accountable.

To my friends, old and new: you inspire me every single day. Every conversation, every email, every text, and every LinkedIn message motivates me to do more, to share more, and become more. It may feel like a drop in the ocean for you, but it means the world to me.

Thanks also goes out to Simha Saida, Dina Shoval, Hadar Sabag, Shani Broner Barkan, Barak Orenstein, Sophie Bonnet, Michael Seiler, Noa Shinar-Ron, Sharon Langer, Michal Bloch-Ron, Yonit Soloducho, Roy Geva Glasberg, Inge Lammertink, Anna

Rosenberg, Omri Aloni, Noa Aharon, Leora Bachrach, Vlada Alexandrov, Karin Noa Frishberg, Austin Belcak, Jonathan Javier, Linh T. Tran, Jonaed Iqbal, Anastasia Ecin, Brandon Dell, Daniel Bottero, Lizzie Ann Jones, Scott Barker, Kyle Coleman, Feren Calderwood, Kenneth (Kenny) Dugger, Cache Duininck, Sara Pion, Saketh Turlapati, Faye Wai, William Laast, and Nair Vineet.

Lastly, to everyone who picked up this book because they know, deep inside, they are meant for more: you are right.

INVALUABLE

Who is Maya Grossman?

Maya Grossman is the author of *Invaluable: Master the 10 Skills You Need to Skyrocket Your Career*. She is a marketing executive, a blogger, a speaker, a podcast host, and a career coach.

Maya is a marketing consultant who works with startups and Fortune 500 companies to help them build high-performing marketing teams. Earlier in her career, she was the VP of Marketing at Colu, a Fintech startup that delivers mobile payment solutions. Before that, she led Product Marketing at Microsoft and was the Head of Digital Marketing at SodaStream, a consumer goods company that was acquired for $3.2 billion dollars. Previously, Maya was an executive director at an award-winning PR and Social Media agency.

Throughout her 15-year career, Maya was able to work for companies like Microsoft and Google, receive multiple promotions and raises, and strategically level up from an individual contributor to a VP. The experiences and the insights Maya gained led her to write this book because she believes that everyone can benefit from developing an invaluable mindset—especially people who are earlier in their career and need the tools for success.

Maya is known for her motivational, authentic voice and her pragmatic approach to career development. Her love for helping others has led her to become a mentor and career coach, and it is one of her biggest passions.

Stay in touch with Maya via:

- LinkedIn: https://www.linkedin.com/in/mayagrossman/
- Her website: https://www.mayagrossman.com/
- YouTube: https://www.youtube.com/mayagrossman

Made in the USA
Las Vegas, NV
05 January 2021